Sisters Are
Cashing In

Sisters Are Cashing In

*How Every Woman
Can Make Her Financial
Dreams Come True*

MARILYN FRENCH HUBBARD

A Perigee Book

A Perigee Book
Published by The Berkley Publishing Group
A division of Penguin Putnam Inc.
375 Hudson Street
New York, New York 10014

First edition: January 2000

Published simultaneously in Canada.

The Penguin Putnam Inc. World Wide Web site address is
http://www.penguinputnam.com

Library of Congress Cataloging-in-Publication Data

Hubbard, Marilyn French.
Sisters are cashing in : how every woman can make her financial dreams
come true / Marilyn French Hubbard.
p. cm.
Includes index.
ISBN 0-399-52572-6 (tp)
1. Afro-American women—Finance,
Personal. 2. Investments. 3. Money. I. Title.
HG179.H825 2000
332.024'042—dc21   99-047185
                                                        CIP

Printed in the United States of America

10 9 8 7 6 5 4 3 2

This book is dedicated to the memory of my mother and father, Lester and Mabel French, with love.

Contents

Foreword

ESTHER GORDY EDWARDS
CHAIRMAN AND CEO, MOTOWN HISTORICAL MUSEUM

MARILYN French Hubbard has the ability to bring women together. When I first met Marilyn in the late 1970s, she was busy pulling together a group of women for an entrepreneur's conference. The conference was extremely interesting, truly enlightening and groundbreaking. Marilyn and the organization she later founded, the National Association of Black Women Entrepreneurs, have had a great impact by helping provide thousands of women with information about owning a business. Marilyn, as an energetic business owner herself, also confirmed for a new generation that they *could* go into business for themselves. Many did, and the impact of African-American women in business continues.

I believe this, her first business book, will have a similar impact with women who want health, wealth, and happiness in life. With *Sisters Are Cashing In*, Marilyn brings a powerful message to women. Her book also underscores the importance of striving for excellence.

As I read *Sisters Are Cashing In*, I was impressed by Marilyn's effectiveness in getting women to examine what wealth means. I have seen her success with dozens of women who employed her principles. Her coaching and advice for using your own God-given talents, for knowing who you are, and for understanding your purpose also can benefit people.

Marilyn offers many how-to strategies in this wonderful book. The strategies behind her *cashing in* philosophy recognize that people are different. People don't learn the same. They have different reasons for what they do. *Sisters Are Cashing In* can benefit women by allowing each Sister to determine and then follow her own path to wealth.

Marilyn is a pioneer. She always strives to help others, and she has a special gift for and a special commitment to helping African-American women succeed. *Sisters Are Cashing In* is her latest contribution, and I expect the book to continue Marilyn's successful track record in not only bringing people together but also educating, inspiring, and motivating them to achieve excellence.

Acknowledgments

I'VE been able to enjoy the journey that took me to the destination of completing *Sisters Are Cashing In* because I have been blessed with a magnificent support system. I thank God for bringing each one of you into my life. Many of you, knowingly and unknowingly, provided me with multiple sources of love and support. If your path crossed mine within the last two years, either at an airport, a ladies' room, a health club, a seminar, a church, a restaurant, or a checkout line, you heard about "the book." Thanks for showing up synchronistically with the blessing I needed at the time; I'm grateful.

I thank my ancestors and guardian angels: my parents, Lester and Mabel J. French; my grandparents, Curley and Elnora Brown; my uncles, Roy Bates, R. C. Brown, and Chester Horton; my mentors: Thom Cleveland,

Louise Grooms, Jesse Jones, Phyugene Stephens, and Mayor Coleman A. Young; and my dear friends Mickey Baltimore, Jimmy Demps, Paul Dunigan, Clyde Giles, Rose Smith, and Julie Chenault Woods. You are not here with me physically, but I continue to be comforted by the spirit of your unconditional love, guidance, patience, and understanding. Thanks for believing in me and my dreams before I believed in myself.

Thanks to my family and extended family: the Bates, Browns, Bransons, Burkes, Greens, Santees, Hortons, and Ropers. Special thanks go to my sister Janice Roper and my nieces Stacy Jackson and Sabrina Thornton for your continued love, support, and understanding throughout the last two years. Paul Anthony Hubbard, thanks for being my wonderful son and a daily source of inspiration to finish the book. Thanks for looking for ways for me to market *Sisters Are Cashing In* and keeping me focused by constantly asking, "Mom, when will you be done?"

I thank my literary agent, Denise Stinson, for presenting me with the opportunity to write this book. Thanks for being a professional businesswoman and being my advocate throughout the project. You are a blessing. I thank my friend and writing coach, Teresa Blossom, for her writing skills, creativity, and technical expertise which guided this book from start to finish. I appreciate your calmness and focus under the pressure of meeting "the deadline." Thanks for making my dream come true. Sheila Curry, my editor at Perigee, a division of Penguin Putnam Inc.: Thanks for believing in my work and guiding me through the literary process in such a positive and professional manner. You are a first-time author's dream.

Thanks to my cousin Ronnie Brown and Jean Melton Thomas for transforming my home office into a functional, beautiful, and peaceful writing environment, and to my medical doctor, Dr. Shari Maxwell, for keeping me healthy.

Thanks to longtime supporters of me and the National Association of Black Women Entrepreneurs in alphabetical order: Betty Appleby, Barbara Atkins, Sharon Banks, Otheia Barnes-Kennedy, Deborah Smith Barncy, Judge Wendy Baxter, Donna Beasley, Bernadine Beaumont, Helen Booker, Lou Bouks, Marsha Brogdon, Janet Brooks, Dorothy Brown, Eula Brown, Incz Brown, Judy Bryant, Rene Bundy, Velva Burley, Judge Wendy Cooley, Claudia Corbin, Harriet Cosby, Lee Craft, Deborah Cupidore, Audrey Davis, Joyce Davis, Dr. Bernadine Denning, Francine Dent, Peggy Dunigan, Marcia Dyson, Lorrine Edwards, Connie Evans, Dr. Dawn Francis, Fannie Gardiner, JoAnn Gibson, Glenda Gill, Verna Green, Beverly Harris, Carol Harris, Dr. Marjorie Lewis Harris, Erma Henderson, Ramona Henderson, Alexis M. Herman, Cheryl Hilliard, Kaaron Hughes, Bobbie Humphrey, Teola Hunter, Phyllis Hyman, Patricia Johnson, Vivian Johnson, Diana Jones, Theresa Jones, Inez Kaizer, Carolyn Cheeks Kilpatrick, Willa Mae King, Rosetta LaMar, Vern Little, Helen Love, Linda Lowrey, Sharon Madison-Polk, Julianne Malveaux, Bella Marshall, Paulette Martin, Gail Perry Mason, Gloria Mayfield, Barbara McCants-Hill, Jamara McNeil, Sharon Morgan Miller, Lorraine Morris, Lucille Morris, Cathy Nedd, Beatrice Nivens, Carmen N'namdig, Paulette Nunley, Joan Parrot-Fonseca, Francine Peguas, Pamela Perry, Acquanetta Pierce, Barbara Proctor, Annette Rainwater, Brenda Rayford, Pat Reese, Rose Reese, Leslie Renzie, Doris Rhea, Dorothy Riley-Green, Pam Rogers, Sheila Rogers, Gail Ross, Kay Russell, Patricia Russell-McCloud, Leslie Sabbaeth, Carolyn Shelton, Sandra Simon, Naomi Sims, Patricia Smith, Mona Lisa Spears, Bobby Joe Stovall, Carma Thomas, JoAnn Virgil, Sherry Washington, Fannie Watson, Loretta Watson, Patricia Hill Welch, Denise White, Janet Williams, Margo Williams, and Barbara Wilson. Thanks for being role models for *Sisters Are Cashing In*.

Thanks to my sisterfriends who are always ready and willing to help me make the impossible happen: Pat Beane, Mildred Birch, Lexcie Blockett, Barbara Branklin, Carolyn Branson, Jacqueline Braxton-Wallingford, Connie Bush, Betty Canty, Nancy Davis, Eddress Dennis, Deborah Dolman, Anita Edge, Elizabeth Field, Debbie George, Lenora Hayes, Denise Henderson, Dorothy Henry, Joyce Huggins, Elaine Ivery, Patricia Jacobs, Jessica Jefferson, A'Lynne Jenkins, Lenora Koyton, Barbara Littles, Sam Love, Gwen Manning-Jones, Shirley Montgomery, Cheryl Moore, Sarah Morgan, Patricia Murphy, Connie Murray Cole, Barbara Niman, Betty Nixon, Karen Norman, Faye Paige-Edwards, Brenda Peek, Yone Peyton, Cheryl Price-Dickerson, Theresa Redden, Dr. Mary Rogers, Marie Simon, Beverly Smith, Georgie Solomon, JoAnn Watson, Minnie Wilson, and Gloria Wooten. We did it again.

To my Brothers and Sisters, coaches, consultants, and professional colleagues: Gerri Barrons, Rev. Linda Beatty, Kelvin Boston, Rev. Sandra Bracey, Dr. Toni Breen, Les Brown, Deborah Carter, James Carter, George Davis, JoAnne Edwards, Elsie Finn, George Fraser, Noel George, Vera Gilford, Celeste Gilmore, Pat Moore Harbour, Mary Horton, Dr. Jeff Howard, Gwen Hurst, Tony Ingraham, Kay Iwatta, Linda Jackson, Kaaron Johnson, Tommie Jefferson, Kenneth Kelly, Renee Killingsworth, Adeligha Lee, Carol McCall, Kevin McCarthy, Carole Mullins, Julie O'Mara, Doris Perry, Jackie Phillips, Tish Preston, Barbara Leftwich Reed, Denise Roberts, Dr. Mary Rogers, Dr. Vaperdeal Sanders, Beverly Scott, Barbara Stambridge, JoAnn Steward, George Subira, Dr. Stuart Taylor, Dr. Roosevelt Thomas, Bill Wells, Mary-Francis Winters, and Dr. Orien Worden. Thanks for lending me your ears, shoulders, and hearts while providing me with your expertise, advice, prayers, and counsel.

To my mastermind partners: Vernice Davis Anthony, Lee Crawford, Deborah Scott, and Cynthia Taeug. Thanks for being my confidants and providing a safe place to share my dreams, aspirations, and goals, as well as my troubles and triumphs.

Thanks to my past and present clients, employers, employees, co-workers, and all of the men and women who have participated in my workshops over the past twenty-five years. Thanks for sharing your stories and insights. A special thanks to Judge Henry Szymakski and my team at Health Alliance Plan and the Henry Ford Health System: Don Davis, Cleve Killingsworth and Fran Parker, Lesia Martin, Greg Johnson, Patty Durr, Lauren Fulks, MaryJo Morelli, Lynne King, Earline White, you have been some of my best teachers.

Thanks to my brotherfriends who continuously support me and my endeavors in their own special ways: Anthony Abernathy, Roosevelt Adams, N. Charles Anderson, Judge Alex Allen, Charles Allen, Mayor Dennis Archer, Duane Ashley, Don Barden, Bob Beatty, Bill Beckham, Dave Bing, Wade Briggs, Bill Brooks, Ken Brown, N. Z. Bryant, Gerald Buchanan, Fredrick Burke, Rudy Colemon, Don Davis, Tommie Dortch, Larry Doss, Walter Douglas, Dennis Dowdell, Larry Drake, Joel Ferguson, Rogers Foster, Al French, Ray Fritz, Robert Gibson, Lloyd Gite, Herman Glass, Delbert Gray, Marcus Gray, Elliott Hall, Ron Hall, Sammie Hall, Alonzo Harris, Angelo Henderson, Rollin Henderson, Sam Hopkins, Paul Hubbard, Rev. Jesse Jackson, Sam Jenkins, Bill Johnson, Daryle Johnson, George Johnson, Oscar King, Phillip Lenud, Sam Logan, Richard Lord, Akim Martins, Howard Mills, Ray Parker, Dr. Bill Pickard, Phil Pierce, Robert Polk, Tom Porter, Judge Jim Roberts, Roy Roberts, Jim Robinson, Don Scavella, Gerald Smith, Calvin Stephens, Greg Wallace, George Walters, Walt Watkins, Eric Wilkins, Greg Williams, Mike Williams, and Wally Williams. Thanks for caring about the welfare of your Sisters and sharing your wisdom and resources.

I thank Martha Jean Steinberg for being "The Queen" and Rev. Charles Adams, Rev. Keith Butler, Rev. Jessica Ingraham, Dr. Don Scavalli, and Marianne Williamson for your spiritual guidance and introducing me to the princess versus queen concept.

I thank my mentees: Paula Brinson, Sandra Brown, Brenda Hemphill, Beverlin Hill, Cassaundra Rice, and Cornellia Shipley. Thanks for believing in me. You are real special to me.

To Oseola McCarty, who passed away as this book was in production, and who remains an inspiration to us all.

To the reader, thanks for reading this book. I hope you enjoy reading it as much as I enjoyed writing it.

Marilyn French Hubbard

Prologue

ALEXIS M. HERMAN
U.S. SECRETARY OF LABOR

As Secretary of Labor, one of my top priorities is making sure every American worker can look forward to a secure retirement. People should get the dignity they deserve after a lifetime of work.

Sisters, that is why the message of saving for a secure retirement is one we at the Department of Labor have been driving home since starting our own retirement savings education campaign three years ago. Our campaign educates Americans about the importance of saving for retirement and helps America's workers to know their rights when it comes to their pension plans.

We are convinced there is a need for education because of a few simple but startling facts: Only two out of five Americans know how much money they'll need to retire. And one out of five Americans has saved nothing for their retirement.

When it comes to African Americans, the picture is more troubling. Only 44 percent of black workers participate in employee pension plans, compared to 51 percent of whites. In fact, while white participation in pension plans edged up from 1979 to 1993, our participation continues to slip.

If we are going to enjoy true economic security throughout our work lives and into retirement, we must turn the statistics and our financial behavior around. Every African American—from the boardroom to the mail room, and every cubicle and corner office in between—must understand that secure, employer-provided pensions and individual savings are a must. Along with Social Security, they form what we know as the three-legged stool workers can rely on once they stop working.

That is why the department's campaign features Oseola McCarty as one of our "super savers." Ms. McCarty washed clothes for seventy-five years and never earned more than $10 a bundle. Yet she saved $280,000, and gave $150,000 of it to the University of Southern Mississippi for a scholarship fund. Her example sends a powerful message about how a little bit, saved consistently, can go a long way.

Sisters, we need your help to make sure the success of our campaign continues. I'd like to invite you to help spread our retirement savings message. Whether it's to your families, your friends, in your communities, or at work, you can help us make sure every worker knows the value of putting money away for the future.

If you own or manage a business, provide all your workers with not only a decent paycheck but the opportunity to participate in a secure retirement plan.

If you are a community leader, continue to use your voice to support initiatives ensuring all Americans— regardless of their gender, heritage, income, or education—have equal access to the building blocks for a secure financial future.

Most of all, become a participant yourself in saving for your future.

Now, I know saving is about tomorrow, and sometimes it's tough for families to look beyond today. There are any number of obstacles in the way. But if we all work together—government, business, churches, communities, and families—we can spread the retirement savings message. And we can make sure every worker has the opportunity to make educated choices to build a secure foundation for their retirement.

Alexis M. Herman
August 1999

Chapter One

Creating Freedom, Wealth, and Power

Sisters Are Cashing In is about more than just money. It is about how women can get their lives in order, so they can have the freedom to be who they really are, do what they love for a living, have what they need when they need it, and make a contribution to the success of others. It's about being, doing, and having it all. *Sisters Are Cashing In* shows how to create freedom, wealth, and power from the inside out by integrating business and spiritual principles that focus on the mind, body, and spirit.

Sisters Are Cashing In will help you become free of worry about money and the financial bondage of having to work long and hard, and of having unnecessary expenses and uncomfortable debt. It is about creating a wealthy lifestyle free from the debilitating fear of losing your most cherished possessions that can be taken away from you by a fire or natural disaster, or the insecurity that can come from building your life around a job that can be lost through corporate downsizing. You will discover how to use money for happiness and fulfillment rather than temporary, fleeting pleasure. You also will stop using a lack of money as an excuse for not reaching your financial dreams. In the end, you will develop a sense of personal power, and your leadership will inspire and empower others.

HOW *SISTERS ARE CASHING IN* WAS DEVELOPED

About twenty years ago, I founded the National Association of Black Women Entrepreneurs (NABWE), an organization for Black women in business for themselves. I personally felt the need for the organization because I owned my own court reporting firm and found very few resources for Black women entrepreneurs. NABWE became an important resource and support network for many women, and eventually served as a template for other women's organizations.

When we had our meetings, women in business or interested in being in business shared their problems, challenges, successes, fears, and tears with me. Some would call wanting information about the Small Business Administration (SBA), and we would also talk about their families, poor credit, divorces, and anything else that was bothering them. I was also a leadership and business development consultant and trainer, so my experience made me a good listener and coach. Black women entrepreneurs, professionals, and corporate executives were not as common then as they are now. So, no matter what the problem, the women I spoke with felt excited and happy about their lives and the possibilities ahead of them because they were pioneers. They drew energy and purpose from doing something groundbreaking, important, and meaningful.

Over the years, I noticed a common theme emerging in my conversations and interactions with women in the business world. Many felt that although they seemed to have it all, they still wanted something else; something was missing in their lives. They were asking, "Is this it?" Or they were saying, *"There's got to be a better way."* There were other women who couldn't figure out what they wanted. They were going from job to job, trying to find something more than they had. And there were those who had an inkling of what they wanted and how to go about it, but they feared they were in too much debt to even think about any new or creative venture. Some even felt that they did not deserve to have their dreams come true. All of these women had skills, education, and abilities to generate money, and were doing so successfully on various levels. Some ran their own small businesses. Several were high-ranking executives who oversaw major corporate divisions with multimillion-dollar budgets and dozens or hundreds of employees. Many had successful two-career marriages and wonderful children. Others were on the fast track in their chosen field and single by choice. Many were doing exactly what they'd dreamed of back in grade school or in their college dorm rooms. These were women who took good care of themselves on the outside, were well dressed and well groomed. They appeared to be perfect role models for success. Still, all these women complained that something was missing from their lives. Some fought confusion; others battled depression as they wondered what they could do to make their lives feel as complete as they appeared.

I began to share with them the experiences, principles, skills, and behaviors that worked in my life and in the lives of other Sisters who had found lasting fulfillment, rather than temporary gratification, while living their dreams. Much of what I shared with them came from experiences and decisions made in my own life, as well as from my education and training in personal and professional development. I shared career decisions I had made and how I came to make these decisions. I also shared the commitment that I had made to NABWE and its members. In the early years, much of my income went into the organization to keep it going. There were hard times: A White House invitation to meet with the president created the dilemma of putting the funds together for a trip that I couldn't turn down. But I was doing what I loved. I was doing what I believed in. I was on a mission. NABWE was my ministry, and that made everything worthwhile to me. It was vital to feel good about myself as a person, and I was committed to getting up each morning prepared to give my family, friends, clients, NABWE members, and others my best in every way.

The women I spoke with drew inspiration and empowerment from what we shared. Then they started referring others to me for the kind of coaching and inspiration that had helped them sort through crises in their lives. Coaching helped them define or redefine what they truly wanted to be, do, and have, and to identify the short- and long-term actions and activities that would produce the results they desired. These women found that they could begin to truly love themselves just the way they were, enjoy their work, their success, their relationships, and their lives. They realized they could have enough money not only to satisfy their needs but to satisfy their wants, too—some for the first time ever or for the first time in a very long time.

It quickly became apparent that women have questions, doubts, fears, and challenges in common that make our lives feel incomplete or unfulfilled, regardless of how much money we have. It does not have to be that way! For every woman who expressed dissatisfaction, I knew other women who were happy and thriving. The key difference between the two groups was that the unfulfilled women believed money or a man could buy or bring happiness, and the fulfilled women believed they contributed to their own happiness.

Sisters Are Cashing In is about finding that fulfillment on the inside. Your true self dwells on the inside. Your most honest thoughts, feelings, needs, and dreams are there. Your talent and other natural attributes spring from there, too. Inside is where your roots are, and they need to be tended and nutured with actions and pursuits that are consistent with your true self. This is often called authentic self-expression. When you ignore the roots of your authentic self or fail to tend to them properly, dissatisfaction takes hold and begins to wither your perspective, your spirit—indeed, your very being. Fulfilled women get that way by tending to their inner selves. Women who believe that grabbing onto money or a man will bring happiness do not get it. Even when they have huge bank accounts or good men in their lives, they remain dissatisfied. If they have no man or no money, they blame the lack of it for their problems.

One of the things I quickly discovered in working with businesswomen is that dissatisfaction or lack of success doesn't stem from a lack of money. Statistics bear this out. Sisters control or influence almost $400 billion as consumers. Sisters make money; they just don't hold onto it or manage it well. The problem is their attitude toward money and how they use it. Many spend to feel better about themselves, and go deeper and deeper in debt. They don't acknowledge the problem until they are seriously out of control, barely making it week to week, living hand to mouth, and robbing Peter to pay Paul. It becomes a vicious cycle: mounting debts affect self-esteem; they need to do something to enhance their feelings of self-worth; they buy more. They spend their cash or run up their credit cards. I believe there is a real connection between the way women work, the way they earn money, and the way they spend money. A Sister who is in a job that does not use her natural talents and abilities does not view her money with the same care as a Sister who is doing the work she loves. A Sister whose actions are not consistent with her beliefs or principles finds that money brings her no joy. Although Sisters control vast amounts of consumer dollars, internal factors contribute to mismanagement of those resources and leave us mired in poverty or a long, long way from our dreams.

Mismanagement is only one part of the unhealthy relationship that we have with money. Women need to start facing their finances in a conscious and consistent way. We need to give ourselves the luxury of not having to think about money so we are free to live our dreams, and are free from undue fear of poverty and isolation or destitution in our old age. Because of our poor relationship with money, we often live with poor financial, emotional, and physical health, feeling stressed, depressed, and sometimes hopeless. We spend all or most of the money we earn to slowly pay off debts. Too many of us have almost no money to provide us with our basic needs now and in our later years. According to national figures, Black women live longer and die poorer than any other segment of the U.S. population. Thus, some Sisters are cashing out, not cashing in.

We can change that. Sisters are better educated today than ever, with a record number graduating high school and college. We have more resources and opportunities. We have come a long way! There are more women on the Black Enterprise 100 List, in corporate boardrooms, and in the U.S. Congress. Sisters like Oprah Winfrey, U.S. Secretary of Labor Alexis M. Herman, Maxwell House executive Ann Fudge, Microsoft millionaire retiree Trish Millines, *Essence* editor Susan Taylor, Johnson Publishing President Linda Johnson Rice, author Maya Angelou, and many other leading Sisters are among the major players on the national and international scene. We have the power and resources to change things so we can enjoy our lives. And because Black women are often heads of households, when we lift ourselves, we also lift our families and our communities. By acting now, Black women can live wealthy and healthy lives in the new millennium.

WHAT *CASHING IN* MEANS

The philosophy of *cashing in* is simple. *Cashing in* means investing in yourself and your future. A Sister who cashes in feels good about herself, her life, her work, and her world. *Cashing in* helps Sisters perform with purpose and passion in all their roles: mother, wife, lover, daughter, sister, niece, granddaughter, worker, boss, executive, entrepreneur, voter, volunteer, community leader, and everything else. In every role, the *cashing-in* Sister knows and achieves what makes her healthy, wealthy, wise, whole, complete, and fulfilled. She has ended her poor relationship with money by putting money into its proper context within her life.

This peace of mind and ability to manage money is available to all Sisters who are willing to do some work. You need only to be honest about what your dreams are, assess how far you are from those dreams, and determine what is needed to fill the gap. You can then develop a plan to bridge the gap between where you are now and where your dreams are waiting for you, then keep working your plan until you reach your goals and cash in.

Now, when most people talk about cashing in, they mean taking advantage of something, like an event, an opportunity, or, sometimes, a person. That is not what we're dealing with here. As you work your plan to cash in, you embark upon what I call a "wealth-creation journey" that enables you to gain both inner and external wealth. This journey will require you to believe in four basic principles that put joy in your daily life. Those four principles are love, energy, authenticity, and purpose. We have to love ourselves as we truly are, have energy for what we do, be authentic in our approach to life, be true to our word, and have a purpose and dream that make us want to be bigger than who we are, to achieve something that benefits more people than just ourselves. Together, these principles form the acronym LEAP, and you must take a leap to start you on your way to *cashing in*.

This book introduces you to women who have cashed out and many who are cashing in. Women who are cashing in do so by building their internal self first. They find their identity and value in themselves, not in money or external items. Women who cash out are on a money-go-round, where emotional baggage from the past weighs down their resources so that their money takes them in circles. They are constantly chasing money to have it, run around spending it, and chase it again to try and clear up debt. Those who cash out have allowed money to define who they are and what they are worth. Some of them are overearners: Sisters who earn money at the expense of others. Some are underearners and underspenders. Underearners are Sisters who don't value themselves enough to put the proper price tag on their abilities and don't earn what they are qualified for and worth, or who are struggling to gain skills and knowledge they assume they need rather than tapping into their God-given skills, talents, and abilities. Underspenders are Sisters who deny basic wants and needs because they don't feel entitled or deserving.

The Steps to *Cashing In*

Through a series of eight steps, this book shows what women can do to cash in. Those steps are See, Surrender, Shift, Simplify, Structure, Support, Share, and Shape the Future.

See: In the Seeing step, you will closely examine the reality of your world and the world around you. Many women have blind spots. They cannot or will not see the truth. Others have blinders that prevent them from seeing it. Blind spots and blinders can also hide your dreams from you. Sometimes, it's easy to lose track of your dreams in the routines of daily life. Can you see your dreams? Opening your eyes to the truth is the first step in seeing your dreams and making positive changes in your life to reach them.

Surrender: The Surrendering step helps you start this journey from where you are right now. You learn how to stop being a victim and how to stop beating up yourself for past mistakes. Think of it like this: There is probably something in your garage or in your closet right now that you could give away and never miss. However, because you hold on to it anyway, you can never make space for something new and wonderful. In Surrendering, you learn how to let go of bitterness, shame, guilt, regret, or how to accept them. Letting go or accepting frees space to allow new, positive things to come into your life as you embark upon your wealth-creation journey.

Shift: In Shifting, you will look at the difference between a Sister and a "Sista" to discover why some Black women live wealthy lives and others do not. A Sister will *be* committed to *do* what it takes to *have* what she wants. A "Sista" talks about what she wants but doesn't do anything about it, so she doesn't have anything. Choose to be a Sister, not a Sista.

The difference between being a Sista and being a Sister is a lot like the difference between a princess and a queen. Like a princess, a Sista is a girl who knows that she will get there, and is on her way, but has not arrived. She has power, but does not use it responsibly. She is often passive and petty. A Sista does not know how to learn from her pain or how to use her pain creatively. Instead, she uses it spitefully or destructively.

Now, a Sister is a queen. She is wise. A Sister has earned her serenity—it has not been bestowed on her—by having passed a personal challenge test. She has suffered and grown more beautiful because of it. Like a queen, a Sister has proved she can hold her kingdom together. She has become her vision. She cares deeply about something bigger than she is. She rules with authentic power. She realizes that one Sister's success is all Sisters' success, and she celebrates herself and others instead of criticizing and being jealous. A Sister works collaboratively with men and other women to forge partnerships and strategic alliances that benefit everybody.

To be a Sista is to play at life. To be a Sister is to be a serious player in life, playing to win, while having fun. In Shifting, you will begin to recognize strengths that will help you go from where you are to where you want to be, and areas that you will need to improve on to make that transition.

Simplify: Simplifying requires you to clearly identify your goals, wants, and dreams. Simplifying helps you to become uncluttered and sharpen your focus so that you can align your actions and activities to support your goals, wants, and dreams. The alignment occurs in the twelve key areas of your life: personal, interpersonal, organizational, spiritual, financial, mental, intellectual, emotional, physical, political, legal, and technical. Everything you do and need to handle falls into one of these areas. Some overlap while others stand alone. There might be times when one area takes on a higher priority than another. The birth of a baby, for example, puts more emphasis on the personal area and less on the job or organizational area during a maternity leave. By simplifying, you can achieve proper interrelatedness and balance among these areas.

Structure: Structuring helps you plot the route to accomplishing your goals and dreams. Structuring makes you accountable. Structuring helps translate what you want and need into actions and behaviors. It also looks at how to measure your progress and to be accountable for your results. If your goal is to complete a college degree, there might be things you need to do before you attend your first class, so that you can earn the grades required. You might need to use time management to add hours for class and study or arrange to have someone take over a time-consuming chore, like grocery shopping or cooking. Structuring starts with such basics, and helps you eliminate excuses and remove obstacles that impede progress.

Support: Supporting might present the biggest challenge for Sisters. Because women are used to going it alone or being the primary giver, we do not ask for help easily. I was like that for many, many years until I realized you go only so far independently, yet the sky is the limit when you work with another person or with a team. Partnering or collaboration allowed me to work with people who had expertise that I lacked and who were able to gain from my knowledge and experience. *Cashing in* is best achieved with company. There are many people you can support and whose support you can request. Everyone needs outside help and expertise sometimes. There is no shame in needing support. This step shows how to recognize when you need a helping hand and where to go for coaching and assistance.

Share: Sharing is an important part of *cashing in*. It includes tithing your time, talent, and treasures to help others. People get a special delight from giving of themselves and knowing that their contribution made a difference in someone's day or life. The joy can put a bounce in your step and make you more positive and productive.

Shape the Future: You help shape the future by involving your children in the lessons of *cashing in* and by leaving a legacy for them. Even young children can begin to apply the principals of love, energy, authenticity, and purpose in their own lives. Through your example and teachings, they also will learn the proper context for money. It is through Shaping the Future that you help break the cycle of generational poverty.

These eight steps are necessary to help you get unstuck and out of your rut, and to help you move to the next level of self-fulfillment, completion, and wholeness. All the steps require that you understand what your dreams are, so that they come true through the work you do. The steps also challenge you to think about freedom, wealth, and power—often in a different way than you are used to thinking of them.

In *cashing in*, you will seek the kind of wealth that springs from the very depths of your soul and washes your life in bliss! Women don't have to wait for someone else or something else to achieve wealth. Women make themselves wealthy by harnessing their personal power. The power comes from being true to your personal beliefs, values, and talents by expressing them in your actions.

In many instances, you must change what you do so that you can produce something different, better, or more. Change takes the old and fixes it. But sometimes change isn't enough and transformation must occur. Transformation is reinventing some of the old that worked and creating something new. Henry Ford could have changed the wheels on the horse and buggy; instead, he transformed it into a horseless carriage. To successfully cash in, you may need to reinvent yourself first. Reinvention draws on the past and the present to shape a new future.

Cashing in does not require you to be a financial wizard or even to have money in the bank. You can start this journey with the money in your purse right now. *Cashing in* requires you first to enrich yourself—your mind, body, and spirit. In many ways, *Sisters Are Cashing In* is about the core spirit, strength, character, and knowledge that we must have inside ourselves before we can start to give and get what we want and need from life. Material wealth is an outgrowth of inner power, not the source of it.

COMMITTING TO *CASHING IN*

To get the most from this book, you have to determine that the cost of getting what you want is worth it—the possible gains, issues, roadblocks, disappointments, and such. You have to be more than interested in *cashing in*. You have to be committed to *cashing in*. Committed to do what you say, regardless of feelings or circumstances. You might need to make sacrifices now to get what you want later. Will you give up an hour of TV to work on a personal development plan? Will you delay a shopping spree to invest in a class that upgrades your skills? Will you put aside baggage and blame that you've carried for years? The bottom line is, pay the price now or pay the penalties later in life with poor health or unfilled dreams. *Cashing in* will require an evaluation of yourself and of your roles and responsibilities as you create a new and better world for yourself.

Ask yourself, What's next? What future do I want to create? What's my dream for the rest of my life? How can I live my dreams? What do I want to give the world? What is holding me back? Is it me?

Remember that the wealth you achieve through *cashing in* is a wealth that is spiritual, emotional, physical, and mental as well as financial.

Sisters have the power. You bring valued diversity to Corporate America. Your skills, ideas, and talents make businesses stronger. You represent a huge consumer market. Companies want you to spend your money on their products and services. Information is also power. When you know how powerful you are, you can use the power to make your financial dreams come true.

START *CASHING IN* NOW

A banner that hung across the entry hall in my son's elementary school proclaimed, *Your "I Will" is more important than your "IQ."* This statement underscores how determination and commitment can help any person achieve great and sometimes unbelievable feats. To paraphrase that banner, *Your "I Will" is more important than your "Income."* Whatever amount you have in your purse right now, you have enough to make your financial dreams come true, because *Sisters Are Cashing In* will help you develop into a woman who can build wealth by leveraging your existing resources. Begin from where you are right now and work to have a breakthrough to your next level. Do not judge your future worth by the money in your purse. Madame C. J. Walker became the first self-made female millionaire in the United States, and she started her empire with less than two dollars.

Money did not finance her dream. Love, energy, authenticity, and purpose did. Madame Walker took the LEAP; you can, too.

I Am on the Journey, Too

My first job after high school was as a secretary at General Motors Corporation. Even though I didn't quite understand it at the time, I remember the pride my family and extended family shared when I attained the title, "one of the first Black female secretaries for the General Motors Corporation." At eighteen, I was more interested in money than milestones, and soon after my first paycheck, I realized I wanted to do something different with my life. Because I could type and take shorthand, a friend suggested that I become a court reporter, because the job paid "a lot of money." That was all I needed to hear. The prospect of "a lot of money" motivated me to change careers, and I enrolled in college for the courses that would make me a court reporter. I met the requirements, and the state of Michigan issued me a license as a Certified Court Reporter. The money began rolling in. Besides getting a salary, I earned fees for transcripts. Attorneys ordered lots of copies, and I got to charge for every page.

However, I didn't like my 8–5 court reporting job. It boxed me in too much. I loved to talk and interact with people—things court reporters do not get to do since most of the job requires listening to testimony, creating an accurate record of proceedings, and making transcripts. With each passing year, I grew more unhappy and felt unfulfilled internally. When I tried to explain my dissatisfaction to my family and friends, most of them felt no sympathy for me. They saw me as making—and spending—lots of money. Based on what they could see, I had no reason to complain. On the inside, though, I felt trapped. I didn't really enjoy my job anymore, but I needed it to pay my bills.

After several years, I realized that I wasn't doing what I loved to do. In order to do what I enjoyed, interacting with others, I started teaching court reporting at a community college and attending career development seminars. The seminars helped me realize that I was doing court reporting just for the money, and what I truly loved was working more directly with people.

I quit my job and opened a court reporting firm, which allowed me to interact with people because I was managing a business, not taking testimony and doing transcripts.

I've been on a perpetual personal and professional journey for almost three decades now. In the process I've studied many business and spiritual philosophies, earned three business degrees, and been honored to share my beliefs in seminars and workshops with thousands of women and men across the country. On the journey, I've learned to accept and love myself by honoring and sharing my God-given skills, talents, and abilities while loving, teaching, inspiring, and empowering others in my work and in my life.

I continue to learn lessons as I serve in the competitive business world. I've learned that personal and professional mastery go hand in hand when you want to achieve the best performance for your life and your bottom line. A mastery in both brings a sense of effortlessness and joyousness, which stems from your ability and willingness to understand and work with the forces around you. Personal and professional mastery are major ingredients in creating wealth and making your financial dreams come true.

My growth and development continue to be shaped by my life experiences. Through the years, I have learned to stay true to myself while accomplishing results and building relationships. Often, that means I am viewed as independent, sometimes as too independent, by people who want me to participate in things that I consider more political than ethical. But it has given me freedom, wealth, and power. I know who I am and what I stand for, and I am consistent in my beliefs and actions. Because I am on the journey, I continue to be tested, too.

Several years ago, I was talking regularly to a friend about some uncertainties he was experiencing in his life. He was in love with a wonderful woman. He had questions about building and maintaining a relationship. When he turned to me for coaching, I referred him to a particular seminar series I had heard about. He wanted to know if I had attended them. My response was, "I don't go to those kinds of seminars; I conduct them." It was a very arrogant reaction, but I truly felt that way at the time. I had been a professional trainer for years. While a seminar on new training disciplines or business topics might interest me, another seminar about relationships did not. But as we talked over the next several weeks, my reaction changed. I came to see that he and I shared some issues that created unnecessary stumbling blocks in our lives.

Eventually, I went to the same seminar series that I'd recommended to my friend. It was a perfect format for exploring issues that I'd buried inside myself. It also reminded me that we all need help and support from others sometimes. You see, although I appeared successful to the world, there were things inside myself that made me feel less than successful and that kept me from enjoying my success. I needed to spend as much time on personal mastery as I was spending on professional mastery, not only to reach my dreams but to live them.

My ongoing growth and development led me to the *cashing in* philosophy. Unless we have love, peace, and joy inside us, we cannot have freedom, wealth, and power. My reason for writing this book is to share that important message. When my message helps one Sister, who in turn helps another, I will have achieved my purpose.

I invite you to come along on the wealth-creation journey with me. You will find it helpful to keep a journal as a record, because this journey will be the catalyst for an extraordinary difference in your life. The journey will require reflection, introspection, action, and transformation. It will help you to reconnect to your lifelong dreams, to what you really wanted to do, be, and have before you lost your dreams in the struggles for daily survival.

My belief is that wealth, freedom, and power are available to everyone. I have consciously been on the wealth-creation journey for almost three decades, and yes, Sisters, we have made progress. In the 1970s, we were focused on surviving. The economic recession made it a hard time for most of us, whether we were working for others or working in our own firms. In the 1980s, we were surviving and succeeding. The economy had picked up, and strong affirmative action programs made government agencies and Fortune 500 companies provide real opportunities to women, Blacks, Latinos, and other minorities as employees and as business owners for the first time. In the 1990s, we were making success happen. We put the first Black woman in space—Mae Jemison— and in the U.S. Senate—with Carol Moseley-Braun. The twenty-first century, the new millennium, will be the era of enrichment for us. It will include transformation and contribution as you bring other Sisters and family along on the journey. Only by working together can women build community and a new spirit, new care, new communication, new commitment, new strength, new conviction, and a new attitude as more Sisters start *cashing in.*

Chapter Two

❦

How You Can Cash In

EVERY woman can have the kind of wealth that comes from feeling good about herself, her life, her livelihood, and her lifestyle. *Cashing in* results in that type of wealth. It makes you feel so good on the inside that your face glows and your actions shine. *Cashing in* ends the emptiness you feel because it requires you to be who you truly are and to act authentically in all you do.

KNOWING YOUR DREAMS

If someone asked you right now, *What are your dreams?*, you could probably give an answer. You might tell about your dream house, car, or vacation. But are these things your *true* dream?

Dreaming is a way of seeing your ideal future. In your dreams, you look the way you want, you act the way you want, and you do the things you want. You are happy, giving, loving, and beloved. You have the family, friends, and community you want. You have the personal and professional resources to support your lifestyle, contribute to the community, and leave a legacy.

Take a few minutes now to consider what your dreams are and what they include. What city do you live in? Who are the people around you? How do you feel? How much money do you have? What are you doing? The details are important. In your journal write, "My Dream is" with as many details as you can.

Once you have written down the details, consider the scope of your dream. Run it through your mind, like a movie. Then, ask yourself:

— *Is this dream possible?*

— *Is this dream worth having?*

— *Will this dream get me what I really want?*

— *Does this dream involve work or sacrifices that will make the dream lose appeal?*

— *Is this dream big enough?*

— *Can this dream be shared?*

Each woman may answer the questions differently. Just bear these important issues in mind:

- If you know someone who is living this dream or if the circumstances exist to support it, the dream is possible. If you don't know someone who has achieved your dream, do some research to assess the potential for making your dream come true.

- The *cashing-in* dream is not selfish, harmful, or spiteful. It is generous, inclusive, and beneficial.

- Dreaming frees the imagination to conjure things that are fantastic and wonderful—but those things still need to be connected to the reality of what you want and need. A dream of career success, for example, will not automatically make your parents or children love you. Know what you want, but before you pursue a dream, figure out what desires, needs, emotions you are trying to fulfill with that dream.

- The Bible asks, "For what will it profit a man, if he gains the whole world and forfeits his soul?" A dream might require hard work and sacrifices, but it should not require you to act without integrity or result in massive costs or damages to health and relationships. Attaining your dream should result in fulfillment and satisfaction. If it doesn't, the dream did not contain the things that you truly needed or wanted.

- A dream needs to be big enough to hold all that you want and need. Do not hold back from dreaming out of fear or past disappointments.

- A dream that helps you work toward the life you want can help others, too.

In many ways, a dream is like a wish—the possibility that something might happen. The difference is the separation between wishing for the dream and wanting the dream. *Wanting* it helps you transition into making a commitment and acting to get the dream. Wanting propels you into action.

Put your dreams to the test by asking the six questions on page 24. Depending on the answers, you may need to refine your dreams. Once your dreams are clear, you can take the appropriate steps and actions toward making them come true. Unless wishing becomes wanting, your dreams will just be part of your imagination. It is only through wanting that you begin to act. Otherwise, getting what you want remains solely dependent upon luck. It does not matter how badly you want what you are dreaming of or how creative you are about devising ways to reach your dreams. As long as you do nothing, your dream remains a distant wish.

ACTING UPON YOUR DREAMS

Now that you have written at least a first draft of what your dreams are, you have started to create an outcome for yourself. Through the steps in *Cashing In*, you will begin to break that outcome into the actions you must take in order to obtain your dreams. Before you get to those steps, you will need to know and understand some of the challenges and issues you may encounter on the way to achieving your dream.

Create the Future

It has often been said that the best way to predict the future is to create it. This means you envision what you want you and your life to be like ten, twenty, or even fifty years from today. To make it come true, you must engage in the behavior and activities that will get you there.

Do you believe you have the ability to create your future? As a matter of fact, you play the most significant role in the design of your own life.

Take a minute to predict the future: It is Wednesday morning, and your dream is to have a weekend free of chores. Will it happen?

Yes, if you use the three days to create the future. During the three days before the weekend, you might add the weekend chores to your daily tasks, ask family for help, or hire a cleaning service. If you don't, your prediction will not come true because you have not engaged in the actions to create it.

Just as you have the power to create your future or dreams, you also have the freedom to rearrange, expand, or change your goals and aspirations. You can even start all over if you choose.

Creating your future opens up new possibilities. The important thing to realize is that you have the choice. You make the decisions. You begin by taking a stand and actually declaring the dreams you want and then being willing to act consistently with that stand. Creating the future takes attention, commitment, and action.

Don't Make Money the Issue

We give money too much power in our lives. We give money the power to make us secure, happy, healthy, successful, sexy, beautiful, popular, powerful, relaxed, or smart. When we lack money, we feel exactly the opposite of those things. In reality, money, in and of itself, does not have that power. We have all heard stories about people who had a dream and little or no money but still achieved the dream. The money was less important than their determination and commitment to their future. On the flip side, we've also heard the stories about millionaires who felt something missing in their lives or who went bankrupt spending money to fill emotional voids. They bought fifteen cars, twenty houses, a hundred gold chains, or some other amazing quantity of some *thing*, but the things they bought were never enough. That's because power is really in us, not in the money. But because most of us have a bad relationship with money, we need to change that relationship so that money stops being a barrier to our creativity and dreams.

When you are creating your future, you will need to release your preconceptions about money. Again, don't discount the future you desire because you don't have money now. That's merely an excuse. Remember that success and happiness are not automatic results of having money.

You have the ability to create the resources you need

or the option to form strategic alliances with other Sisters to leverage your resources. When your dreams have abundance, you begin to create your future by believing in abundance, not scarcity. Also consider the possibility that money "flows" for worthy goals. Banks, foundations, and other lenders consistently back people who have a clear vision of the future and projects and products that will contribute to society.

Discover the goals behind your desires for money. What do you want to be, do, and have? Then find ways to meet those goals while spending less money—or no money at all. Once you discover the essence of what you want, there may be other ways to meet those goals than spending money.

Know the Meaning of Key Terms

One of the symptoms of a bad relationship with money is confusion about key money terms like "income" and "wealth." They are not the same. Income is what you earn. Wealth is what you accumulate. Wealth does include fulfillment.

You might also confuse "wealthy" and "financially secure." Financially secure is having the long-term money to secure your future, but it may not include the fulfillment and happiness of your preferred future.

Here are other common terms that are often confused:

Rich and Poor: Rich is having money but not necessarily having wealth. Rich may include getting a windfall of sudden money like an inheritance, lottery payout, or insurance claim. It is often temporary because there is no plan for investing the money or putting it in balance with other areas of your life. Poor is more than not having money. It includes not having the attitude of a person who is capable of generating money.

Fortune and Fame: We often think that if someone is famous, then he or she must have fortune. That is not always the case. When Rosa Parks got mugged a few years ago, the public was surprised to learn that her principal income came from her job as a congressional aide. It paid less than $60,000 a year. Sammy Davis, Jr., was near bankruptcy at his death from cancer. It wasn't that he did not make money; he had not managed his money.

Affluence and Influence: Opinion leaders like presidents of trade associations or professional societies and many politicians have influence over community and national issues. But most draw an ordinary paycheck. A church minister also has great influence, but often must have another full-time job to make ends meet. Unpaid volunteers of community organizations also can be influential people.

Affluence reflects an attitude of history, traditions, and culture. Affluent people send their kids to the "right" schools. They are well-traveled and have good taste. They often live in upper-middle-class neighborhoods. Their incomes range in the high five figures or the low six figures. There are usually two such incomes in their households.

Wealth and Power: Both H. Ross Perot and Steve Forbes are billionaire businessmen. Through their corporations, they wield considerable power in the economy. Yet, despite spending several million dollars out of their own pockets, neither man did well during presidential elections. Remember Jimmy Carter? He was just a peanut farmer from Plains, Georgia—who spent four years as the most powerful world leader when he became president of the United States. What all these men had in common was that they were making a difference while making a living. They were committed to service with purpose, and their lives, lifestyles, and livelihoods supported their purpose.

Use the "Be, Do, Have" Paradigm

You can change the things in your life that make you feel unfulfilled. To change what you are getting, you must change the behavior that brings the unfulfilling results. Computer techies coined a good phrase for this phenomenon: GIGO, which stands for "garbage in, garbage out." It means that when you do not put in the right stuff, you do not get the right stuff out.

The "be, do, have" paradigm means that you need to BE who you are. Know your strengths, weaknesses, and purpose. This self-awareness will lead you to DO what you love. This doing will be the contribution of your unique God-given gifts, skills, talents, and abilities. Because you are giving yourself away, you will be rewarded and HAVE what you need. Most people spend their lives trying to Have enough (money, resources, things) so they can DO what they want (in terms of work, how they spend their time). Once they have achieved that, they think they will BE happy. To turn the having/doing/being cycle around, you have to stop making "having money" the goal. You cannot measure success only by your bank accounts and possessions. You have to get your priorities in order and follow your heart, guided by your values.

Put the Past, Present, and Future in the Right Order

Even as we create the future, we have to live and operate in the present. To reach our desired future, our actions and behaviors in the present have to be aligned with our visions of the future. Most of us, however, base our daily lives on the past. We get caught up in what has happened, not what is happening now. For example, when you were in school, the teacher called on you to speak and all the kids laughed at you. Now you are afraid to speak in public. But let's say you want to be a public speaker. You will need to focus on the present and future instead of on the past. Ridicule for your speaking happened in the past. To succeed with your dream, you need to let go of the past and focus on the future you *want*, not the future that will emerge if present trends, based on the past, continue. When we talk and think mainly about the past, we often repeat the same actions over and over. It has been said that doing the same thing over and over and expecting different results is the definition of insanity. Focusing only on the present with no future in mind also stymies us, because we tend to deal with the activities and challenges of the day-to-day routine without an eye toward moving on, improving, or achieving. This focus doesn't give us the future we desire. Talk about your goals! Share your vision for the future with others! Manage your conversations, what you listen to, watch, read, and think. Move your consciousness to your future.

Putting the past in the past and having the present geared to the future helps us to be proactive instead of always reactive. This allows us to learn from the past, live in the present, and create our future.

Embrace Change, Reinvention, and Transformation

There is a spiritual compass in each of us that helps guide our feet in the path of actions that are consistent with our values and beliefs.

We have to be willing to transform ourselves to create the future we desire. It's been said, *If you keep doing what you're doing, you'll keep getting what you're getting.* You may even have to consider reinventing yourself from moment to moment. If you merely change, you are making an improvement in results that you already have. If you are willing to transform yourself, you will be able to make choices and to create results that do not yet exist. Make a commitment to mastery, quality, excellence, and continuous improvement. If you are not producing the desired results, you have to look at what's missing, not what's wrong. Ask yourself, What's missing? or What am I not doing? Where have I stopped? To prepare ourselves for the twenty-first century, we must give up what is familiar and comfortable, and choose that which is fulfilling, satisfying, and exciting.

Live and Work for a Purpose Higher Than Money

People who become wealthy focus their time, energy, efforts, and money on doing what they love to do. They put their natural talents and aptitudes to work. They learn to listen to their inner voice and their heart's deepest desire. They find the essence of who they are, and share it. The money that comes from that work is a secondary, not a primary, consideration for them. Sisters who live this way open bookstores, not to just sell books but to boost literacy in our communities, to boost knowledge. They go into cosmetics or hair care to make Black America beautiful. They focus on what they love to do and make certain their resources are reinvested in that work.

Having a purpose gives us a meaningful way to live. The purpose can be to add beauty to the world by creating jewelry or gift baskets; to bring financial services to a neighborhood redlined by the banking industry. For you to become truly wealthy, your actions must reflect your purpose, and your purpose must be reflected in your actions. What is your purpose?

Develop an Entrepreneurial Mind-Set

Entrepreneurs are among the most adaptable people I know. They do not fear change; they thrive on it. In the new millennium, there are going to be a lot of changes.

We all must realistically assess our readiness for the new millennium. What skills will the marketplace need? What is the next step as it relates to our future, our work, economic opportunity, and quality of life?

I believe that living in the twenty-first century will take an entrepreneurial mind-set. Operating from an entrepreneurial mind-set will improve your ability to anticipate the future with optimism. An entrepreneurial mind-set is not just about starting a business; it is a way of thinking and behaving. By adapting entrepreneurial attitudes and behaviors, you strengthen the way you operate, the way you serve your customers, the way you meet your goals, and the way you focus upon your individual mission in life. You become customer-minded, always looking for the next need, with new and better ways to fulfill those needs. This creates new or better products and services for companies to provide to consumers, and happier workers behind desks, on assembly lines, and in corner offices.

Sisters with an entrepreneurial mind-set meet the demands of business or enterprise. They also meet, rather than hinder, their own personal needs, values, and goals. If they lose a job, they quickly land on their feet. After exploring their circumstances, they innovate their way toward their next step or option. They realize the world is always changing and understand that to remain competitive, they must change, too. They engage in entrepreneurial attitudes and behaviors: They look ahead. They watch for trends. They plan for change. They do not fear change; they thrive on it because they see it as an opportunity for growth and learning. They are prepared. They trust their intuition and judgment, and are willing to take calculated risks without waiting for the full picture or all of the details. They are committed to the long term and are willing to invest their time and resources, regardless of how much time it might take to go from rough concept to tangible reality. They are willing to rise far enough out of their mental ruts to be able to see new alternatives and opportunities.

Cashing in requires you to become a woman who has wealth in her life, not just in the bank. The journey to this kind of wealth requires a belief in your ability to know yourself and to base your actions on the principles and steps explained here. This includes believing that you can create the future; not making money the issue; understanding the difference between key terms like "wealthy" and "financially secure"; putting the past, present, and future in their right places; living and working for a purpose higher than money; and adapting to the entrepreneurial way of life in the twenty-first century.

❦

Chapter Three

The Power of Change: When Nickels, Dimes, and Quarters Make Women Millionaires

OSEOLA McCarty worked her entire life as a small-town maid. Quitting school in the sixth grade to care for her grandmother, Ms. McCarty cleaned, sewed, and did other chores in Hattiesburg, Mississippi. She did her work with purpose and pride, using her God-given talents and skills. She did the work she felt she was called to do—and did it with excellence. She earned poverty wages and lived frugally, saving the pennies, nickels, dimes, and quarters that made up her income. Ms. McCarty worked with joy until a few years ago, when she retired at age eighty-six.

Most of us consider what Ms. McCarty did menial work and her pay, small change. Yet, long before she retired in 1995, Oseola McCarty was a wealthy woman:

she had quietly amassed more than $250,000 in savings and lived life as she chose.

Ms. McCarty didn't save a large amount over a short period of time; instead, she set aside a little bit regularly over the years. She also paid her bills on time. The money, though, was never the most important thing to her, because she enjoyed her work and her life. Each day she worked, she did her tasks with peace of mind and an easy heart. She was a lady who knew who she was and who joyfully served others. Ms. McCarty accomplished the most important things she wanted to accomplish in her lifetime. She had the experiences that she wanted, and pursued activities that were important and worthwhile to her. When she retired, she converted her savings into a rich legacy by establishing a scholarship fund for University of Southern Mississippi Black students.

Her unselfish gift brought her national celebrity and even more money. Word of her generosity spread. Newspapers ran headlines with her name. Morning talk shows interviewed her. This woman, who had dropped out before high school to care for her family, even got a book deal! People started referring to her act as "The Gift," and sent money to Southern Mississippi and other organizations. These were not outcomes that Ms. McCarty actively pursued. Instead, they resulted from her simple desire to do the work she loved and to serve others. Her blessings flowed from her personal commitment to be herself.

Ms. McCarty and I met one winter in Detroit when

she was in town to promote her book, *Simple Wisdom for Rich Living.* I saw a woman who had lived life on essential levels and lived it well. She had grown up, gone to work, taken care of her family, paid her bills, worshiped her God, and grown older in good health. She valued and took time for her family and community. Her work had meaning. She said she started each day on her knees in prayer and meditation. While she worked, she had fun. She sang and told stories. She always had enough money. She did not waste anything, nor did she deny herself. She bought what she wanted. When she bought clothes, she bought items of high quality. She looked good and felt good. She kept things as simple and as organized as possible. Ms. McCarty didn't believe in long-term credit. If she used it, she put half down and paid the balance off right away. She planned for the future. She put money in the bank, where it compounded interest, and left her investment alone long enough for it to increase. Over ninety years old when we met, she remained in good health. Before we parted, she told me she still had a lot of learning to do. She was looking forward to her future!

Randye Parker, forty-four, is a technology sales representative who has earned at least $100,000 annually for the last twelve years. She regularly exceeds quotas and sets new records. Her company acknowledges her with certificates, plaques, and expensive gifts and trips as the "Top Salesperson." A college graduate, she owns a condo in suburban Detroit and escapes the bitter Michigan winters with trips to Hawaii and other tropical locations. Randye hates her job, but she keeps it because she is driven by the financial rewards that come from sales. She feels tired and stressed at the beginning and end of each workday.

Randye has little to look forward to. Her work has no meaning for her except the paychecks. The plaques and certificates that she gets as a top sales performer do not make her proud because she takes no pride and finds no joy in what she does. She undercuts and does things that she is not proud of, like padding expense accounts, for the almighty dollar.

If Randye loved her work, understood what she wanted from life, and knew what to do with her money, she could be wealthy, too. Instead, Randye is often broke, emotionally and financially. The clerks at the local pawnshop know her personally. They also know her fur coats, her diamond rings, and her other valuables. By her visits, they know when her condo or car payment is due. Despite her six-figure income, Randye struggles to pay gas, telephone, water, and light bills. She is a conspicuous consumer who spends everything she earns, and then some, on unnecessary, frivolous, and disposable items. She does not control her money because she cannot. Randye has not come to grips with the reasons she spends money the way she does. Her wasteful spending stems from having something missing from her life. No matter what she buys, it is never enough to fulfill her. Her inability to control money creates emergencies that need not happen. It also prevents her from enjoying life and planning effectively for the future. Friends call her a "drama queen" for her maneuvers to keep one step ahead of bill collectors who want to repossess her latest car or cut off her power, phone, and cable TV.

Randye also operates a small, home-based catering business, which contributes at least $15,000 to her annual income. She loves doing it, and she's great at it. She uses some of her family recipes, like Big Mama's Plum Roll and Aunt Annie's Apple Cobbler. Although the thought of using a family legacy is appealing, she dismisses it because she does not believe she can make the same money from catering that she makes in sales. So she doesn't invest any time or effort in her small business. She takes on projects only when she needs extra cash in a hurry. Although she loves cooking and catering, she is driven primarily by the need to earn quick money that she can go spend right away. She has not thought about what she wants from life, how to make the most of her God-given talents, or what she needs to do to have joy in her life each day. She is not willing to do the soul-searching or the planning to be true to herself.

Too many women are like Randye Parker and too few like Oseola McCarty when it comes to using our talents and resources to build wealth for ourselves. We don't invest in ourselves or in our futures. We don't do the work that brings us joy, yet we get little joy from the work we do to bring us money. Too often, we are worrying about not having enough money for the week or dealing with short-term crises that sap our energy and prevent us from planning and preparing for the long term. We may let our emotions shape our attitudes about money and about the way we earn, save, and spend money. Unable to reign in these attitudes, we don't take the time or the control to create the future of our choice. We don't plan to take the necessary daily steps and critical actions that maximize our well-being, labors, and worth. Without taking the time and planning, we cannot cash in later for a wealthy life that includes joy of living, working, and being in the world.

CASHING IN VS. CASHING OUT

Ms. McCarty is a great example of what this book means by *cashing in*. She is wealthy in every way that counts: She has peace of mind, purpose, satisfaction in her daily work, and all the money to do what she wants. Her financial wealth flowed from the joy she got by living life her way. She knew what she wanted, and she was true, or authentic, to herself in the way she went about achieving what she wanted. She is wealthy, but her wealth isn't tied to the money she has.

Randye is an example of cashing out. All the money she earns has not satisfied her in any lasting way. She also illustrates why it is not advisable to define wealth solely by money.

Cashing in does not equate wealth with money. Neither does it confuse wealth with money. *Cashing in* is about freedom, about setting ourselves free, not just from debt and financial worries but also from the weight pressing on our shoulders, spirits, and souls. Sisters desperately need to be set free. We have been enslaved for centuries by the shackles of low expectations, abuse, discrimination, fear, racism, sexism, and more. But there is nothing that we can't overcome. No matter where we are in the world, we can free ourselves from what keeps us from our dreams.

Cashing in is a way to invest in ourselves and our futures and to maximize our value, worth, and contributions. *Cashing in* means recognizing that we have choices: We can control our lives or money can control our lives. We make a choice to live in wealth, to live in poverty, or to live enslaved to the gods of consumerism. Investing in ourselves puts us on the path to freedom so that we can live the life we freely choose, a wealthy life. *Cashing in* is recognizing we can use our knowledge, skills, and abilities to make a better life—and do it on our terms.

Cashing out means relying on money to solve all our problems. By believing money can solve everything, we become willing to do almost anything to get it. We act without integrity. We do things that disagree with our beliefs. We take a job we hate. No wonder people cashing out have stressed minds and crushed spirits.

Your inner strength, drive, and determination are worth so much more than the amount of money that you have or earn. *Cashing in*, in the right way, requires you to know yourself more and better than you do right now. You must know what your principles are, what you believe in, what you stand for, what you want from life, what will make you happy, what will energize you to get out of bed each day. You have to ask yourself, and answer honestly, *What do I want my life to be like, and what do I need to do to make it happen?* Too often, we dream about what we want, but we don't follow through to determine what we are willing to do to achieve our dreams. Dreams come true because we have clearly defined what needs to be done and have completed the actions that are critical to achieve them, not because we go out and buy them.

TAKING CARE OF YOURSELF

Women are accustomed to being the primary caregivers in the family. That is an important and noble role in the American and world culture. Too often, though, a woman will spend time taking care of others while neglecting her own needs to such an extent that she requires medication, bed rest, or hospitalization.

It is necessary to remember that you can nurture others and still take care of yourself. Take a moment to think about how well you take care of yourself at the internal level—your emotional and mental wellness. Ask yourself:

— *Do I set aside time for myself?*

— *Is meditation, prayer, or silent contemplation a part of my daily routine?*

— *How often do I converse with myself about my feelings, my needs, my dreams?*

— *When do I nurture and feed my spirit?*

— *What do I do to feel a part of the world? How do I prepare myself to participate and make a contribution in the world?*

This internal soul-searching is important because these questions will help you to determine what you can offer the world. By putting your personal development first, you ensure that when you do reach outside yourself, you can give your life great meaning and joy.

With her six-figure income, Randye has not figured out any of the requirements for a fulfilled life. She is taking the unproductive approach. Randye is trying to *buy* a lot of dreams. She indulges her impulsive, fleeting wants, and her life looks good—on the surface. She has fun, but it's temporary, and she pays for it by feeling stressed and depressed and by hiding out from creditors, often in the dark because the electric company has pulled the plug. By spending all she earns, she will have to work beyond retirement age whether she wants to or not.

Randye is driven by a pattern of behavior that is part of her bad relationship with money. She admits that the way she spends money is crazy, that it plunges her into debt and leaves her depressed and feeling stupid for wasting money. But she doesn't know why she can't stop doing what she's doing.

Randye has not realized that she can have the same lifestyle she has now—trips, parties, shopping sprees—without the drama and without risking her health, credit rating, reputation, or future. She has not examined the reasons and behavior that cause her to throw money away, so she will not be able to change her behavior. Having to hide from bill collectors is not enough of a financial breakdown for her to end her pattern of reckless spending and consumption. She says she is interested in changing, yet she is not *committed* to making a change.

She does not really want to delve into defining or clarifying her inner resources.

Not all of us are in the same hole as Randye. Some of
us are in ruts and some of us are in trenches. But none
of us are in so deep that we can't get out, and neither is
Randye. We can get unstuck from where we are.

Cashing in is a journey to achieve wealth in your life.
The wealth we want includes self-expression, freedom,
and power, not just money. If money were all it took to
be wealthy, a six-figure income would buy a lot of
dreams. With a six-figure income, any woman would appear to be positioned for financial wealth, for becoming
a millionaire through a strong savings and investment
plan. But sales professional Randye has been earning that
for years, and she's not living her dreams, nor is she
headed for wealth. She is headed for financial and emotional bankruptcy because she does not know what she
wants or needs from life, and has no long-term commitment and plan for her money or her life. *She does not
know what she wants to offer the world or what she wants to
accomplish in her lifetime.* A small-town maid, Oseola
McCarty, obviously had a plan and stuck to it, choosing
to live prudently in order to achieve her plan because
she was committed to it. She exhibited a discipline directly opposite Randye's recklessness. As a result, Ms.
McCarty started with small change—nickels, dimes, and
quarters—and ended up wealthy, while Randye is often
broke.

We don't have to live at either end of the spectrum
to get what we want from life. In fact, most of us fall
between these extremes. Wealth can be achieved from a

range of incomes and by a range of different women. The chapters ahead show how to start on the inside so that you can make the most of investing your time, energy, and, yes, your money to consciously create the future you want and make your wildest dreams come true. It's easier to get what you want when you know what it is.

❦

Chapter Four

Your Relationship with Money: Understanding Past Influences and Present Behavior

To fully understand *cashing in*, you need to put money in perspective. Money is an important tool to use to achieve financial dreams. But, before you can use it, you will need to understand what money can and cannot do for you. Most people have a poor relationship with money because they place tremendous, often impossible expectations upon it.

Look at it this way: More than 1.5 million retail stores operate in the United States. We have some 1,500 malls and shopping centers where we can shop until we drop, and when we drop, we can now shop on the Internet and via television. Still, despite all the goods and services for sale in America, there is not a store where any of us can buy happiness or wealth.

However, we want—and even need—to believe that

money will solve our problems. People with money have it all. They cannot be unhappy, right?

Wrong. People do not become happy or satisfied from having money. You see, money does not and cannot fill the voids inside us, especially those voids that stem from unfulfilled inner needs. There are hundreds of stories in history and even in today's headlines about rich people who were not happy or who felt something important was missing in their lives. They've had prestigious names like Vanderbilt and Duke or royal titles like the Princess of Wales. There are also ordinary people you encounter every day who have money but don't have happiness.

One is Amy, a woman I've known since high school. Amy became financially secure when her father died in an accident. Amy's father was a high-ranking corporate executive who started his career by selling insurance. He believed in his product and was very well insured when he died. As a result, Amy is one of the richest women I know. She also is one of the unhappiest.

As the insurance payout climbed past a million dollars, Amy got scared. She began to worry that everyone would be after her money. Since she had no other close family, she moved to a small town where no one knew her. She got a job that she didn't really want and didn't really need. Going into a funk, she gained some fifty to sixty pounds. These days, she frequently travels alone because she cannot find anyone to go with her: Her friends with money don't have the time, and her friends with time don't have the money. She sees gloom and doom every-where. When we get together now, Amy has become such a killjoy that she depresses everyone around her.

Able to live a luxurious lifestyle on just the interest from her money, Amy is financially secure, but not wealthy. She has not *cashed in*. Her money has become an anchor. It weighs her down with suspicion, doubt, and unhappiness. Part of the weight may stem from her grief over her father's death, along with some guilt that she got the money only because he died, and feeling she doesn't deserve it. Amy denies that, of course. She says she loved her father, but adds that she is over the grief caused by his death more than a decade ago. Yet, after more than ten years with more money than she ever imagined, she is still not fulfilled. She can do anything she wants to do, go anywhere she wants to go. But something inside of her is holding her back from getting freedom, wealth, and power. Until she can identify what is holding her back she can't conquer the problem, and Amy will never know true wealth. She will continue in her cycle of gloom and doom, confused about why her life is not what she wants it to be, and feeling powerless to change it. So she goes on another month-long cruise or engages in some other activity that makes her feel good and fulfilled for a while. But those activities don't fulfill her: They all are subconscious delaying tactics that allow her to avoid dealing with the root causes of her unhappy feelings and the real reason she feels unfulfilled and powerless to change her life.

THE MYTH OF MONEY

Because the myth of money is so powerful, it is important to examine more closely the role of money in society, including the way today's popular culture measures wealth, because it establishes a standard for success. Money has a tremendous influence on the careers we choose, the houses we live in, the cars we drive, the clothes we wear, and other decisions that outwardly showcase success.

Society's standards for measuring success not only feed the collective standards about wealth but also influence individual perceptions. Often it is the struggle to reach or keep up with society's standard that creates challenges. Not every woman wants or needs the things deemed essential by popular culture, but that does not necessarily stop her from pursuing them, which can lead to frustration and disappointment that can prevent her from *cashing in*.

First, let me remind you: There is no lack of money among Sisters. Some 8 million work, with 1.6 million in high-paying managerial and professional jobs. During 1999, highly educated Black women helped drive expected spending power of African Americans to a record $533 billion, a nearly 73 percent increase in less than a decade (which opened with $308 billion in 1990). The increase for African Americans was significantly above the 57 percent increase for the entire nation. Women controlled more than half of this amount and influenced a large quantity of the rest. More than 300,000 Black women—one in twenty-six of the 8.3 million Black female labor force—bring home $50,000 or more in annual income. We do not lack money.

What we lack is a good relationship with money. The way we view money affects the way we handle money and partly determines how we spend and save money. Some women have mixed emotions about money. Perhaps as children, we saw our parents working too hard and struggling, hardly making a dollar. Others of us were influenced by the Great Depression or other hard times. Many of us have misinterpreted the Bible passage about money being the root of all evil, and rejected money for religious reasons. But the passage says the *love* of money is the root of all evil. Others embraced the declaration made back in the 1970s by the flamboyant Reverend Ike that "the lack of money" was the real problem. Different factors can influence our feelings about money and help set the stage for our poor relationship with it.

Many women have a very poor relationship with money because they do not have a good relationship with themselves. When they feel insecure, they put diamonds in their ears and gold chains around their necks—like sales diva Randye. They spend money to give themselves an emotional boost. They spend money to ease the pain of hurt feelings. With their skewed view of money, they try to buy things that make them look good on the outside when they feel bad or empty on the inside.

They also tend to hang in the wrong circles. Their friends and shopping buddies are women with similar bad habits. These Sistas only reinforce poor relationships with money.

Feeling empty or unfulfilled is common among women. The reasons vary, but they all create identifiable, common patterns for how women see money, what they do with money, and what they expect money to do for them. They see and use money as a substitute for the fulfillment that they want to have inside. Money also becomes a tangible expression of power, a symbol of value to the outside world. Money becomes the shield that hides feelings of inadequacy, hopelessness, and powerlessness. Some women believe a mink coat can cover a lot of scars. But the mink coat doesn't make the scars go away.

Let's look more closely at the reasons behind the scars, the reasons women often feel unfulfilled in the first place, and how those reasons lead them to spend money to try to fill the void.

Feeling worthless. As young girls, women may have been told by adults—parents, aunts, uncles, teachers—that they weren't important, or treated that way. They may have been called names like *ugly*, *darkie*, *fat*, or *stupid*—and it stuck. These words could have come from well-meaning relatives who were teasingly showing love in the only way they knew how. But the negative feelings created by these words can last a lifetime. For some women, the feeling of worthlessness comes from suffering physical or sexual abuse. These women carry the scars into adulthood, feeling soiled, molested, unvalued.

Feeling unloved. Sometimes Sisters are looking for love in all the wrong places. Because of a lost love or feelings of rejection from past experiences with family, friends, employers, or relationships, they are not able to put love and passion in their lives, lifestyles, or livelihoods. Sometimes they feel unwanted and uncared for. In romance, women go searching for their other half, not realizing that two halves may not necessarily make a whole. They don't understand that they have to be whole themselves. The feeling of being unloved and lonely can be depressing and an energy drain on our minds, bodies, and spirits. When this happens, the need to be loved blocks us from being all that we can be by ourselves.

Feeling unworthy. Women usually feel someone else is more deserving than themselves. This is part of women's self-sacrificing character. So what if a woman polished all the pews, cleaned all the windows, ordered flowers for the pulpit, vacuumed the carpet, and cut the grass at the church? God deserves the credit. It's the house of the Lord. She was just helping out. Ever try giving a Sister a compliment? It's a hard thing to do. Tell a Sister her hair looks good, and she'll say her stylist does such a good job, or she has her grandmama's "good" hair (whatever that means). Because women do not feel worthy, they have a hard time accepting a simple compliment, much less a bounty of richness.

Feeling unqualified, not good enough. Many women believe that only the very best and brightest are in charge of things and that this group knows what it's doing. If women had power, they would only mess it up. This attitude allowed women to languish in the shadows of men for so long. Many women believed that men knew better and knew more (forgetting men were the ones who told women that!). Even those women who have let go of that myth still haven't let go of the feeling that others are qualified, but they aren't.

Feeling inadequate, not enough. This is the "one more" syndrome. We need only one more piece of furniture to make the house look finished. Unfortunately, when that piece is purchased, we'll still be looking for one more thing. Or there is one more seminar to attend, one more book to read. Women need one more month, or one more day, to get something done right. The problem is that there is always one more thing, and women feel inadequate as they chase it.

Feeling hopeless. Many women look at the barriers created by sexism and racism and think, *Why bother?* When they try to share their dreams with others, they are told "get real" or are asked, "What's for dinner?" They feel invisible and misunderstood.

These feelings are at the root of bad spending habits. Women use money to try to soothe these feelings. Spending money also helps them to deny these unhealthy feelings and this emptiness. You've probably heard many times that you should not go to the grocery store on an empty stomach, because, if you're hungry, you'll put more food in the shopping cart and spend more. Much of the extra food is junk food that is high in fat, sugar, or salt—things that lack nutritional value. Well, Sisters, internal hungers make us do the same thing. To fill our internal emptiness, we spend money and load up on a lot of junk that leaves us broke, with nothing of value to show for it.

Are you starting to see the role of money in your life? Are you starting to see more clearly why you should not rely only on money to make you happy? If you are, then you are creating the kind of mind-set that will help you cash in. If you aren't, I urge you to honestly examine whether you should start a wealth-creation journey, where money is not the primary designation.

Women cannot achieve wealth until they deal with the feelings that skew their relationship with money.

PARENTS, EVENTS, AND OTHER THINGS THAT SHAPE OUR RELATIONSHIP WITH MONEY

Think about what money has meant to you in the past. What were the conversations about money like in your household when you were growing up? I have heard many women say that they grew up with negative ideas about money. For many women, money was something that men earned or handled, and women had nothing to do with it. Men were more financially adept. Or the women saw money as something they did not deserve to earn or deserve to have spent on them.

Some women feared that having money would make them unattractive to men, would make them a threat to a man's ego, pride, or self-esteem. They saw money as gender-related. They stopped themselves from earning a lot of money for fear of losing their sexual attractiveness.

Other women have told me that money was always a survival issue—there was never enough. Each day brought a new fight to get money. It made some women grow up believing in scarcity. To women with a scarcity mind-set, there is never enough money to go around.

They believe that the more you have, the less there is for everyone else. Negative ideas about survival, scarcity, and dependency tend to perpetuate problems. Some believe you have to struggle for money. If it comes too soon or too easily, it can't be real or worth anything. Money has no validity if it hasn't been earned with pain and suffering, with blood, sweat, and tears.

Religious faith exerts a great influence on what women think about money. In the Bible, they read in 1 Timothy 6:10, "For the love of money is the root of all evil: which while some coveted after, they have erred from the faith, and pierced themselves through with many sorrows." Or Matthew 19:24, which states, "It is easier for a camel to go through the eye of a needle, than for a rich man to enter into the kingdom of God." Taking the verse to heart, some women grew up believing that it was better to be poor and righteous than rich and evil. Their religious beliefs also made them believe that the more you suffer, the holier you are. The lack of money actually made them feel self-righteous. People with this perspective usually resent those they consider to be "rich" people. Ironically, it is this resentment of rich people that keeps them poor, because they would resent themselves a lot more if they became rich. I call this the "big shot syndrome." I often hear these self-righteous people (who, I believe, consider themselves "have-nots") refer to people they think have money, status, wealth, or affluence as "big shots." These self-righteous people secretly want all or some of those qualities for themselves, which makes them even more critical of the "haves" because they resent wanting those qualities.

Others have shared with me that their parents were in debt until they died, and the life insurance money solved the financial problems they left behind them. Even though their financial lives became easier because they inherited the money, they feel guilty about having the money because someone had to die for them to get it.

How we look at money is also shaped by what we went through as we grew to adulthood. The Great Depression that followed the stock market crash on October 29, 1929, continues to impact America's social and economic policies. Other views are shaped by people in our childhood. Some of us grew up listening to Reverend Ike, who in the early 1970s had a weekly Sunday morning religious show. It was called *The Joy of Living with Reverend Ike.* To put it mildly, Reverend Ike was a flamboyant man. He drove fast Cadillacs, draped his body with gold chains, diamond rings, and other jewelry, and boasted of his beautiful women. His message from the pulpit was just as flashy. "If you want pie-in-the-sky when you die," he'd declare, "I'm not your man. If you want your pie now, with ice cream on top, then you've come to the right place." Reverend Ike also liked to say, "The LACK of money is the root of all evil." Millions of people tuned in to Reverend Ike, and he influenced how many of us viewed money. He was one of the first media evangelists who shamelessly solicited cash and didn't care who knew how he spent it.

Reverend Ike also used to say, "Money is something like a woman—you have to court money the way you court a woman, and you have to like it. You have to treat it right if you want it to love you." No wonder some of us expect to get love from money.

YOUR RELATIONSHIP WITH MONEY

Money is neither good nor bad. It is energy. It has a spirit that we give it. The way we make and use money determines whether our dollars have positive or negative energy. I once loaned an acquaintance some money, and when she gave it back to me she said, "If you knew what I had to do to get this money, you wouldn't take it." We must attach a level of integrity to what we are willing to do for money. That same integrity should be reflected in our wealth-creation strategies. It is part of forming a better relationship with money.

Money Attitude

Because your view of money affects the way you spend and save money, it is important to understand your attitudes about money. Ask yourself these questions:

— *How do I view money?*

— *What influenced my view?*

— *Has my history with money been positive or negative?*

— *Did I see my parents enjoy money?*

— *What was my first relationship with money? Was it positive or negative?*

— *Did I ever have fun making money?*

— *What triggers my spending?*

Who have been your teachers where money is concerned? Were they people who tried, but never succeeded at investing or making money? Did they treat themselves to anything worthwhile? Did they have a wealthy spirit? How were they with managing their money—paying their bills and making good investment decisions? Sometimes we have had sad people in our lives who didn't feel good about money. How wealthy were they?

Do you sometimes spend money because you feel worthless? Not good enough? Inadequate? Hopeless? Are you able to use money for the good of others or only for yourself, to get more and more for yourself? Is money your primary concern? Did your parents argue about money? Do you have a poverty or scarcity mentality? Do you fearfully cling to money as if you need it to breathe?

Fear is a sign to pay attention. Understanding what you are fearful of can teach you a powerful lesson. We have to put our lives into proper order and *teach ourselves how* to relate to money out of a possibility mind-set. Ask yourself, What does wealth really mean to me? What would it mean for me to behave in a wealthy and powerful fashion?

Once you understand the reasons you feel about money as you do, you can break bad money habits. Instead of going shopping the next time you experience an emotional disappointment, write in your journal about your feelings. You can also estimate the amount of money you would spend and use that money for something else—like paying a bill or investing in a sixty-day certificate of deposit, a savings bond, or company stock. If you still find yourself heading to the mall for a purchase you don't need, go to the nearest park and take a brisk walk. You might also join Debtors Anonymous so you can have a support system that helps you stop needless spending. Or you could consider volunteering at a local charitable organization and helping others instead of store-hopping at the mall.

Be honest with yourself about what triggers your spending. By recognizing the triggers, you can substitute other behavior—physical exercise, creative writing, volunteering—that can help you end your poor relationship with money. As you do, you will start to use money properly.

The proper use of money occurs when it is a tool and resource that moves you closer to your dreams. Using money properly includes budgeting for household and personal items, saving for future needs or wants, and investing in your dreams.

Sisters cannot cash in without putting money in perspective. Money is an important tool to use to achieve financial dreams, and it is a part of creating freedom, wealth, and power. But money does not have magical powers. If we are unhappy because a man cheated on us or scared because our parents lost all their money in the stock market crash, no amount of money will make us happy or secure. Placing tremendous, often impossible, expectations upon money dooms us to a poor relationship with it.

What We Do for Money

Some people believe it is not right to enjoy yourself and get paid for it. *They are misguided.* Work takes up a lot of time and energy and is a major part of how people spend their time, so why not enjoy it?

Your work is an extension of who you are. It shows your excellence and points to the kind of person you are. Martin Luther King, Jr., in one of his many famous speeches, said, "If a man is called to be a street sweeper, he should sweep streets as Michelangelo painted, or Beethoven composed music, or Shakespeare wrote poetry. He should sweep streets so well that all the hosts of heaven and earth will pause to say, 'Here lived a great street sweeper who did his job well.' "

That is the kind of integrity and excellence you and every person need to bring to your work so that you can be proud of your work. You can perform with that kind of integrity and excellence only when you do the work you are called to do.

A national business news reporter once asked me what the secret of success was for entrepreneurs. My answer was simple: *Entrepreneurial people succeed because they do the work they love.* Entrepreneurs are driven by the belief that what they are contributing is the best product or the best service they can deliver. They personally believe in what they are producing, so they accept that breakdowns occur, but they do not interpret breakdowns as failure. They keep trying, investing their talent, time, and resources because they know a breakthrough is just around the corner. They know that when a door closes, a window opens. Financial performance of their businesses is important, mainly because a strong performance means they can keep doing the work they love and not only reap the monetary rewards. Many entrepreneurs become multimillionaires, but they view their *work* as their success and contribution to the world at large. Work to them is a part of serving through using their God-given skills and talents. Work is an integral part of their lives, and their businesses often expand to include their family members. What started as an entrepreneurial venture becomes a family business that gets handed down from generation to generation.

Because work is a primary part of life, it is important for you to gain clarity about the role of your business, professional, or work life. You may try to disconnect from your work when you leave at the end of the day, but this is not possible. Your work or involvement in the business world is integral to who you are. Business and work can be a means of authentic self-expression that is also present in all other aspects of life. The way you live your life is your primary business. You have to remind yourself that money follows, it does not lead. When you put money in front of everything else, it causes confusion in both your personal and professional or business lives.

Some people put money in front of the work, which means they want money and the work is simply a means to get the money. They do not get or give any satisfaction on the job. They do the work they are required to do, but nothing more. Those people who work only for the money have a tendency to create debts and to use installment payments for the things they have bought in an attempt to give themselves the satisfaction that they miss at work, or as a reward for the struggle and pain they believe they endure at work.

To be truly successful, you have to invest in your talents. When you do, you will see your talents multiply. How can you use your natural talents and abilities to create work that you love? Living and working your talents gives you freedom in the area of work, which you need. Otherwise, you will feel unfulfilled.

Tap into your natural talents and abilities, and do what you love for a living. It is natural and fun to express yourself by doing what you love to do. When you do, you don't need competition and the rewards of competition to motivate you to provide your product or service in the world. Who you are becomes what you do.

Many people follow what they love by turning their avocation or hobby into work for a livelihood. The difference between an amateur and a professional is that a professional attaches value and a fee, and receives compensation for the product or service he or she provides or performs.

Doing what you love for a living is inspiring, and leaves you feeling energized and alive. There is a difference between being called and being driven. Being called is putting your natural talents, skills, and ability to work. Being driven is pursuing the almighty dollar rather than doing what you enjoy. Understand that your wealth contributes to your freedom and your freedom contributes to your wealth. Wealth and freedom equal power.

Concentrate on doing what you naturally love to do.

Go to the library and seek information about others who turned a hobby or a vocation into a business. Perhaps you already know a shop that grew from the owner's hobby; stop by (during nonpeak hours, please) and ask the owner how she did it. Visit your local Small Business Administration or Small Business Development Center and look at the collection of business plans. Perhaps one can serve as the template for turning what you love to do into a business!

Work, Money, and Wealth

A final result of a poor relationship with money is the way money, work, and wealth get twisted together in your mind and in your life. Many people believe that hard work is required to be wealthy because their parents came home from work tired every day or worked two jobs to support the family. The focus for most Americans after the agricultural economy shifted into an industrial economy was to go to college, get a good-paying job, and buy a house with a two-car garage in the suburbs. That was the American dream. That was the picture of wealth. What generation after generation discovered—and what helped spark increased entrepreneurial activity in the 1970s and 1980s—was that when we work only for money, money is never enough reward. Yet work, money, and wealth remain twisted in the American psyche.

Doing the work you love is a part of achieving wealth. Wealthy people seek to build a consciousness based on what they want. They look at what's possible and change, reinvent, or transform themselves so that what was once considered impossible becomes possible. They gain knowledge and experience while seeking to educate and expand themselves whenever the opportunity presents itself. They value the opportunity to use their natural talents and skills.

Wealthy people seek first to make a living from what they do, but they do not initially seek to earn millions of dollars. They want to earn an income to support themselves with the work they love. It is their dedication to their life's work that brings them financial security.

Women who achieve wealth do not usually do it overnight. They focus on what they love to do and almost always invest their money in themselves, not in investments they aren't familiar with. They are absorbed in their own work and pursue it consistently and steadily over a number of years. Although they may change careers or directions, their dedication to their life's work brings them financial security.

Wealthy people start out as ordinary people who are happy with themselves. They are self-motivated, creative, and innovative. They function first with purpose and passion. They have self-confidence, skills, and knowledge to achieve what they genuinely want—and they believe they can do it! This prosperous mind-set helps them overcome barriers that can knock other people to the curb.

Finding work that pleases and fulfills them is just as important to them as financial compensation. That's why so many wealthy people are entrepreneurs or have an entrepreneurial mind-set: They go into business to do the work they love. And because money is not their main motivator, they go on to become financially secure.

Microsoft retiree Trish Millines is one example. In the '80s, she took a job at a relatively small and unknown business in the Pacific Northwest because she loved working with computers. She retired from the company as a millionaire at age thirty-nine. She didn't know when she went to work for Microsoft that Bill Gates would build it into the worldwide computer giant it is today. She was doing work she loved, and looked at herself as partnering with the company, not simply as Bill Gates's employee.

Trish Millines left Microsoft a few years ago. She had reached a stage in her life where she was ready *and able* to pursue other dreams. And she knew what those dreams were. According to the *New York Times*, her biggest project is a foundation that she created to help train minority children in computer skills. "We've been really lucky," she said of herself and the thousands of other young multimillionaires created by Microsoft's success. "And one of my first instincts as a person who grew up fairly poor is: You have it, you share it." There speaks a wealthy woman!

Wealth does not come from doing work we dislike or hate in order to achieve a high income. Although they are often confused, income and wealth are not the same. Income is what you earn. Wealth is what you accumulate.

We also confuse being wealthy with being financially secure. Oseola McCarty is wealthy. Oprah Winfrey is financially secure. Oprah has millions upon millions of dollars in the bank and—most certainly—in a diversified portfolio that includes business ownership, real estate, precious metals, stocks, treasury bills, and other investments. Barring the end of U.S. civilization as we now know it, Oprah's money will be enduring.

Actually, Oprah has achieved both being wealthy and being financially secure. Through her popular syndicated talk show, the world has seen her grow as a person and a woman who values herself, loves what she does, and seeks excellence in all she does. If Oprah's bank accounts were wiped out, she could build her wealth again. She has the energy, the passion, the talent, and the commitment to achieve and be successful.

YOUR MONEY RELATIONSHIP

Your poor relationship with money makes you confused about what money really means and what money can do for you. The greatest myth about money is that it will solve all your problems. It doesn't. Also, money alone does not make you wealthy, especially since wealth includes the fulfillment and life pleasure that you desire and need. Many things influence attitudes about money. The Bible, parents, a stock market crash, or a flamboyant TV minister can cast money as evil, hard to get, necessary to hoard, or a cure-all. The standards used by society and popular culture to measure wealth play a part as well. Unfortunately, attitudes about money create behavior patterns that go beyond how money is earned, spent, saved, and invested.

By understanding your attitude about money, you will

begin to see patterns of spending and earning behavior that have kept you from achieving true wealth. By changing your money attitude and your relationship with money, you open yourself up to finding the work you love and the financial resources you need to live the life that is right for you.

Chapter Five

The Money-Go-Round: How to Get Off So Your Financial Dreams Can Come True

REGARDLESS of what has shaped your relationship with money, you may have formed a pattern of money behaviors that I call the money-go-round. The money-go-round happens when money doesn't take you forward. The money-go-round only takes you in circles, away from your dreams.

Poor decisions about spending and not reducing debt send you around in circles faster and faster. You make the wrong decisions over and over again because you have not dealt with the underlying reasons for your behavior—acknowledging what is missing in your life and why you feel unfulfilled, helpless, and powerless to attain satisfaction or happiness.

THE MONEY-GO-ROUND

The money-go-round has four stages:

Stage One: *Sick and Tired*

Stage Two: *Trying (and Failing) to Get Rich Quick*

Stage Three: *Business As Usual*

Stage Four: *Vicious Cycle*

Some of us go through the first three stages in a cease-less cycle. Only breaking the vicious cycle of the money-go-round can free you to be ready to begin a *systematic* approach to building wealth.

Realizing what stage you are in will help you break the endless cycle of spending, accumulating debt, and spending more in a misguided attempt to feel better or fulfill some other emotional or psychological need.

Stage One: Sick and Tired. You are sick and tired of your current situation. You don't have enough money to do what you want. If you have a job, you live paycheck to paycheck. Bill collectors call. Each workday, you drag yourself out of bed in the morning and hate going to your job. You have no energy and no enthusiasm. You feel unhappy and unfulfilled. But you are too much in debt to even think about quitting work or look for an-other job.

Occasionally, you wonder, *Why are other people doing so well? Why am I in this pitiful situation?* Or, *What's wrong with me? What's the secret that I don't know?*

You begin to ask whether other people are prospering

because of their education or their contacts. Did they win the lottery? Were their parents rich? You become more frustrated and sick and tired of your current situation. You can see only the financial responsibilities that make you sick and tired of your life.

You can get out of this stage by:

- Deciding that you want a better life for yourself

- Realizing that if you keep doing what you're doing, you'll keep getting what you're getting

- Becoming more than interested in making changes and becoming committed to changing

- Committing to the actions that make a difference in your life

Stage Two: Trying (and Failing) to Get Rich Quick. In this stage, you look at ways to get rich overnight or as quickly as possible. You become fixed on the notion that all your problems will be solved if you can just figure out how to get a windfall of money, a large lump sum to pay for all your dreams.

In the newspaper, you see great investment ideas—but you can't invest. You have no money. Yet you may be spending $30 to $40 a week on lottery tickets and thousands of dollars on trips to casinos and racetracks. You decide that you don't have to work that hard, not when the Powerball or Big Game jackpot is worth $20 or $25 million this week. So you get right back in line with everybody else trying to get rich quick. You even play the numbers in the neighborhood, or you go to bingo and play ten or twenty boards at the same time.

On television late at night, there are millionaires in infomercials selling books and tapes on how to make money in real estate with no money down. Or how to make an extra $10,000 each month working part-time from home. You place an order for a "Get Rich Right Now" package, maxing out your Visa or MasterCard or spending all your cash. You listen to tape 1 in the series or read the first few chapters in the book and find that the information doesn't apply to you or won't work the way you thought it would. You toss it away or into a corner with all the other "Get Rich Right Now" packages that turned out to be "We Got Your Money Now" experiences.

Another scenario common in this stage: You're approached by a friend at the beauty salon, nightclub, or bar, by coworker Shekieta, or by fellow church member Mark who always has an inside track on the latest multilevel marketing program. They convince you that you have to be in on the ground floor of this exciting opportunity. You join and are able to convince a few other people to join, too. But for some reason, after a couple of weeks, you get bored. You don't know more people to sign up. You haven't become rich. In fact, you've sent more money down the drain and owe more on your credit cards.

In some cases, you may have a dream or an idea of how to get rich by turning your favorite hobby into a business. But you dismiss it because it's *your* idea—not something from a book or an infomercial. Your lack of confidence keeps you stuck.

Often, you decide to wait until the kids get a little bit older *or* until you get a little bit older *or* until you retire from the job you hate *or* until Mr. Right comes along to rescue you. *Then*, you can be happy. Or you get disgusted and complain to everyone you know about how unfair life is. You argue that it isn't fair that some people make all the money. You even blame it on racism or sexism, and produce plenty of data to make your case.

To stop pursuing get-rich-quick schemes and waiting for your life to start until . . . I get the money/man/ideal job, you must:

- Rid yourself of victim mentality and behaviors

- Notice how rarely "get rich quick" schemes work. Open your eyes long enough to see that the people cashing in at casinos, racetracks, bingo halls, and the like are the owners, not the bettors.

Stage Three: Business As Usual. Because so much of our culture stresses instant gratification, when you don't see results of your new financial plan in a few weeks or a few months, you get impatient and feel like giving up. In this stage, you start to second-guess constructive choices that might lead you out of Stage One or Two. You are wondering if financial security is even possible for you, so you panic and scrap your wealth-building plan entirely. You hold back on sharing your dreams. Because the future fulfillment of those dreams seems so far off, they begin to feel unobtainable, and it seems easier to go back to business as usual.

When you let go of those dreams and revert to past behaviors, you may become more self-destructive than before, creating more debt, making more wrong choices, and closing yourself off from opportunities to make positive changes. Saying things like "You only live once" or "You can't take it with you," you spend, spend, spend.

Stage Four: Vicious Cycle. While some women get stuck in one of the previous three stages, others get locked into Stage Four: a vicious cycle that takes you endlessly through Stages One, Two, and Three. You ride the money-go-round faster and faster, moving between the different phases of Sick and Tired, Get Rich Quick, and Business as Usual. Because you try different schemes or periodically work a get-rich-quick plan to improve your future, you think you are doing something constructive to break the cycle and get off the money-go-round. In reality, you are just doing things that keep you and your money from going anywhere but in circles. You repeat the behaviors that doom you and your family to a continuous financial struggle or to poverty, generation after generation.

Being on the money-go-round and behaving carelessly with money can cause embarrassing situations such as eviction, utilities disconnected for nonpayment of bills, inability to buy gifts for special occasions, being denied credit, losing custody of children, and not being able to take care of bare essentials. Behaviors that contribute to creating these situations include:

- Borrowing money from friends and not paying it back

- Using ATM cards for withdrawals without recording the transaction

- Not keeping track of expenditures

- Not paying taxes

- Not paying bills on time

- Spending more money than you make

- Writing checks you know will bounce or postdating checks

- Maxing out on your credit cards

- Putting items on layaway and being unable to pay for them

Many people have shared with me that they are frightened by any mail that looks official or legal. They say they don't like bank tellers, mail carriers, lawyers, or accountants because such people usually give them bad news. They say they don't answer their telephones during the day, or they screen their calls and don't answer any call that is unidentified on their caller ID because it is usually a bill collector. They have negative feelings about the Internal Revenue Service (IRS) and they dread April 15. They say they sometimes have difficulty sleeping because they worry about their money problems. Often, they avoid friends and family because they owe them money and have not kept their promises to pay the money back. They are usually lonely.

Every Sister needs to confront and master the situations and behaviors that keep her on the money-go-round. For most of us, our perceptions, our behaviors, and the way we handle our challenges and opportunities create the barriers that leave us broke. Unfortunately, being on the money-go-round reinforces internal feelings that have a negative impact on our self-esteem, our well-being, and our sense of fulfillment.

Where are you on the money-go-round? Do you see yourself in one or more of the four stages? None of us can make progress in achieving our financial dreams when we base our decisions about money on attempting to fulfill an emotional need or make up for something— self-esteem, love, companionship, safety—that we don't have. Are you cloaking your emptiness by spending money on mink coats, gold chains, diamond earrings, a BMW, or the latest trendy products? Is feeling unworthy or not good enough causing you to miss or turn down opportunities that can enrich you or help you learn new skills? Do those feelings keep you out of the game? You must answer these questions in order to understand what money can and cannot do for you. By understanding why you feel unfulfilled and how it affects your relationship with money, you can make a realistic plan for making your financial dreams come true. Otherwise, you doom yourself to staying in the patterns created by your lack of fulfillment.

The emotional component of our money decisions is undeniable. We Sisters empty our purses and ourselves to serve our families, friends, church, community, and jobs because we want to feel loved, needed, and important. We buy our kids a video game player from every manufacturer and spend $40 or more every couple of weeks to supply them with video games when one player would be enough. Or we buy jeans by a designer who publicly says that he does not make clothes for all people to prove we can wear the clothes. We women spend some $2 billion on our hair and our nails because when we don't feel good inside, we want to look good on the outside. We buy a lot of comfort food to ease loneliness. When it comes to money, we spend to give ourselves an emotional boost, a power trip, and other emotional pick-me-ups.

The financial blues lead to other conditions or problems that sap our energy, motivation, and commitment to change. They affect our health and contribute to obesity and hypertension. According to the American Heart Association, heart attacks and strokes are the top killers of Black women. Yet, the proportion of Black women who reported not doing any leisure time activity or exercise is 39.5 percent, significantly higher than any other race or gender group. Poor financial habits also may be costing women more expenses for mental and physical health care.

Maybe we know what is holding us back from making an improvement in our well-being, but we don't know how to move on or are afraid to let go of the things that are keeping us stuck. There is comfort in familiarity, in our patterns of behavior and lifestyle, even if it means staying in a job we've had and hated for years and years! Sometimes we believe we just have to accept what we have now as permanent. The renowned novelist and playwright James Baldwin once wrote, "Nothing is more desirable than to be released from an affliction, but nothing is more frightening than to be divested of a crutch." A dead-end job or a dead-end relationship can be a Sister's affliction, but she stays with it because it is the crutch she uses to justify why she cannot progress in life. If she changes the job or drops the man and still fails to achieve her dreams, then what can she blame?

Other, less obvious things hold us back. Some of us reach a level of success that no one else in our family attained, and we simply stop reaching. We think we have made it or we think we should be satisfied with making it *this far*. We don't give ourselves permission to reach farther, to go for our wildest dreams or even to dream bigger dreams. If we do dream, sometimes the dreams are small because we have been down in the dumps for so long. We simply don't know how to go about getting past where we are right now.

Sometimes, even when we know what our dreams are, we don't always know how to make them happen. We don't engage in the right habits, or we don't access the right networks, or we don't believe we will truly get to live our dreams. We think we don't have the resources or that it takes a stack of money to make more money. We give up, and lose hope. Sometimes, we believe we're working toward our dreams, but we get sidetracked. We spend our hard-earned money on small items that turn into bigger problems—like paying unnecessary finance charges or late charges because we didn't pay our bills on time, or by impulsively buying things like new shoes we don't really need because we get depressed and shop to cheer ourselves up. We get sidetracked by big things, too, like investing in the wrong kind of mutual fund because we didn't do our homework, or making the wrong choices in personal relationships that drain our emotional and financial resources.

We also procrastinate. In our twenties, it is time to learn about the rules of the financial game, lay the foundation for our financial future, and start to save. But we figure we have plenty of time for that. We focus on getting an apartment, buying our first car, building our party wardrobe, having a good time, and maybe paying off college loans. In our thirties, we should be building on the foundation laid in our twenties. But we're usually trying to scrape together enough to buy a home or to keep our children fed and clothed. Ideally, in our forties and fifties, we should routinely apply what we have learned by making smarter buying and investment decisions and by leveraging our resources. Instead, we start to panic because the time we thought we had is quickly running out. We realize our money has flown out the window in a million wasteful ways. Our sixties and beyond should be the golden years when we enjoy the fruits of our plans, labors, and sacrifices. But unless we act now and set clear goals for each decade of our lives, our golden years are not guaranteed.

Start with the Money in Your Purse

Part of the big misconception about wealth is that you have to have money to achieve wealth. That is not true. Don't get me wrong: money is necessary. We cannot take care of ourselves without money. But money is not the only or even the main component required for you to start your wealth-creation journey.

In fact, it is possible for you to succeed in wealth creation with just the money in your purse right now! I know it is hard, if not impossible, for many of us to see that money does not, and should not, have a primary role in what we are about to undertake. But our history is filled with women who succeeded with little or no money. Many of us have only to look as far as our mothers or grandmothers to see women who achieved much with little.

Some of these women made history. Remember Madame C. J. Walker? She became the first self-made female millionaire in the United States. Guess how much money it took to start Madame Walker on her way to millions. $10,000? $50,000? $100,000? Madame C. J. Walker used a whopping $1.50 to start her hair care business.

Remember educator Mary McLeod Bethune? She started her college for girls with just 15 cents more than Madame Walker had.

A lack of money did not stop these women from achieving their goals. Their desire and their commitment to make a difference were more important than the money in their purses. They were building a legacy or living for a purpose higher than themselves. They were committed to bringing others along as they did the work they were called to do. In the heyday of her business, Madame Walker employed more than 20,000 African-American women in the United States, Central America, and the Caribbean. Mary McLeod Bethune went on to found the National Council of Negro Women. Like Oseola McCarty, these women showed how valuable small change can be in achieving success when matched with the inner commitment to what you believe in and the desire to make a dream come true.

For a moment, though, let's assume that money is necessary to create wealth. If it were, this book would not be necessary! Why not? *Because Sisters, in fact, do not lack money.* That is also part of the misconception about wealth. Whether we realize it or not, a lack of money alone is not our problem. Sisters control or influence some $400 billion as consumers. We spend $1 billion a year just on our nails! That's not a lack of money. Having all that money at our disposal still doesn't satisfy Sisters. What we lack is inner fulfillment, which is more important than money.

Using money as the principal excuse for not striving or achieving stops us dead in our tracks and keeps us from searching for other ways to reach our dreams. But putting the blame solely on lack of money also prevents us from taking a good hard look at what else might be holding us back.

If you have been stuck in some stage of the money-go-round, you can see that going around and around in circles is threatening to your financial dreams. If you want to cash in, this vicious cycle threatens to trip you up and block you at every turn unless you come to terms with it.

Another approach to breaking the vicious cycle is to

consider whether, whenever something happens in the present, you automatically respond and assign a meaning, interpretation, explanation, or conclusion based on the past.

For example, when you were young, you fell down in the middle of the classroom and other kids laughed. At the time you had numerous thoughts and feelings: you were embarrassed, you started crying, you were mad at yourself, you felt like a fool, you were afraid your friends wouldn't like you anymore. Then you formed an interpretation of those thoughts and feelings, either consciously or unconsciously. For instance, "I have to look good all the time if I want people to like me," or "If I don't have everything under control, I'll embarrass myself." That interpretation became part of the road map of your identity; for instance, your priorities became looking good, being in control, and never letting others see you as being vulnerable.

Think back through your past. Identify a significant event that helped shape the path of your identity.

- What happened?

- What thoughts and feelings did you have?

- How did you interpret those thoughts and feelings?

- In what ways are you still acting out of those interpretations?

- How would being able to reinterpret the situation make a difference in your life?

Your transformation will begin by getting off the money-go-round and breaking the vicious cycle of interpretation by distinguishing what really happened from your interpretations of what happened. Consider the possibility that because your identity has emerged out of your interpretations and your interpretations may be preventing you from making your financial dreams come true, you must reevaluate those interpretations and, where necessary, reinvent yourself in order to succeed.

Consider me as your coach or trusted friend to help you through this process. From working with other women and doing personal and professional development, I have found that what is holding you back is usually something that happened in the past—whether it was three months or three decades ago. Many of us have something in our past that sometimes subconsciously prevents us from moving forward. Some of these roadblocks are things that have not been done or things you have been told or how you've been made to feel. They also include promises that have not been kept or college degrees that have not been completed. You may need help in healing pain, you may feel like a failure because of the little promises you have made to yourself and others that you have not kept. Whether the promise was losing twenty pounds, finishing that college degree, or some other goal or project that you started but did not complete, not achieving that goal may have a larger impact on your self-image than you realize.

The way you feel inside has an impact on what you accomplish on the outside. The wealth-creation journey is an inside-out approach. You first engage in personal inquiry—clarifying what you want from life, identifying what you will do to reach your dreams, and defining your goals. The inside-out approach requires personal mastery. Personal mastery is when you are able to live your life without constant struggle and produce the results you want with a sense of effortlessness and joyousness.

One of the outcomes of personal mastery is that you will start to control money instead of having money control you. These are changes that enable you to jump off the money-go-round or to slow it down so you can easily step off at any of the four stages—Sick and Tired, Get Rich Quick, Business As Usual, or Vicious Cycle. You will break through what is holding you back by taking the time to understand what stops you and by coming to peace with these issues or completing unfinished tasks and moving forward.

Chapter Six

The Sister Cashing In: The Qualities of a Successful, Enterprising Woman

THE wonderful thing about *cashing in* is that it can take you wherever you want to go. It taps your personal power to make you a leader in whatever you choose to do. As you seek to make your life wealthy, you need to be mindful that women fill a leadership role by enriching families and communities when we enrich ourselves. That is part of our power.

In October 1996, the National Association of Black Women Entrepreneurs held the first Entrepreneurial Leadership Summit and Conference. A few days after the national mass mailing of the event's brochure, I got an interesting call from a man in New York.

"Your program is wonderful. It's just what people need," he praised. Then he dropped his bombshell, "But

I think you're about five years too early. Women aren't ready for it."

Too early? The words floored me. Based on the research conducted by NABWE before putting together the three-day event, I was confident the caller was wrong about our timing. Technology and economies were changing at warp speed around the globe. Entrepreneurs were creating thousands of jobs and reaping the profits and wealth. However, the Black Enterprise 100 was not growing to the BE 200, and women were not on the BE 100 in high numbers. The revenue, profit, and employment levels of firms owned by Black women in particular were lagging behind the phenomenal success of businesses owned by our white counterparts. If anything, some might consider our timing a bit late.

Soon other responses flooded our mailbox and voice mail. Both women and men were responding positively. Women saw the need for the conference for themselves and their colleagues or friends. Husbands and fathers wanted to register their wives and daughters. People called from growing Sunbelt cities and struggling Rust-belt towns. They called from rural communities and from Canada. Yet, again and again, women who owned or aspired to own their own businesses kept saying, "I want to come, but I'm not a leader."

The repetition of this belief pointed to a lack of personal empowerment among Black women. It became another challenge for conference organizers and for NABWE, which had been championing women business leaders since 1978. The conference tackled the issue head-on. In opening the Summit, the first thing I said was: Become a self-proclaimed leader.

I started as a self-proclaimed leader. When I saw that no networking resources were available for Black women entrepreneurs, I joined with other women to form NABWE. No one stopped us. In fact, it was just the opposite. Government agencies, corporations, community groups, and the media wanted to help us because we were pulling together an audience that their organizations needed to reach.

We are all leaders, and we all can be leaders building wealth and helping other women do the same. Like the women at the Summit and Conference, I want you to claim your personal power and leadership now, and begin to assume that role. One of the things I've learned in life is that you cannot wait for someone to save you. But you can save yourself with your personal power.

Remember, leadership includes sharing the wealth and becoming a coach, mentor, or role model to bring others on the wealth-creation path. It means recognizing the value of our diversity and how our diversity makes a difference in the world. Leadership includes taking a stand and leaving a legacy. Before women can become effective leaders, we must realize our own value and personal power, and, as leaders, help other women see the value and power in themselves.

A Role Model for *Cashing In*

Through working with Fortune 500 companies doing business coaching and training sessions, and running NABWE since the 1970s, I have met some truly dynamic women. They've shared their successes, failures, loves,

and woes from the battle in Corporate America, entrepreneurship, and their other life endeavors.

Another NABWE conference that sticks in my mind
is one we held several years ago with the theme "Black
Women Entrepreneurs: Doing What They Love for a
Living." Sisters came from the north, east, south, and
west. Susan Taylor, Terri Williams, Naomi Sims, Lola
Folana, Phyllis Hyman, Bobbie Humphries, Esther
Gordy Edwards, and other powerful Sisters from around
the world attended. There were Sisters ranging in age
from twenties to seventies. They were successful entrepreneurial women, wanna-be entrepreneurs, on-the-side
entrepreneurs, and other Sisters and Brothers who just
care about the future of entrepreneurial women or like
the enthusiasm and inspiration entrepreneurial women
possess.

These enterprising women love themselves, have energy, express their authentic selves, and proclaim their
personal power and leadership. Over the years, I have
found eight common traits that make it possible for Sisters to cash in, to build lasting wealth for themselves and
their families. These traits fall into eight categories: forgiveness, self-awareness, quality, possibility thinking, interdependence, energy, vision, and adaptability.

As you read through these traits, keep in mind how
you might be exercising these abilities in your life, or
how you may be able to acquire a particular trait.

Eight Traits of Enterprising Women

1. She has the ability to make peace with the past (forgiveness).

To achieve true wealth, you must get rid of the victim mentality. Develop your ability to express yourself fully, so that others relate to you not from your past experience but from the power you bring to the present and the possibility you open for the future.

Creating wealth is a mind-set. You must develop a new perspective. You must be willing to re-create yourself and shift from dependence to independence. You must realize that you have the power *now* to create your life of choice.

A new life can't be created when you constantly focus on the past: looking at the things that you didn't accomplish or the money you wasted. You do not create your life by dwelling on the victim or loser mind-set, or by holding on to old ideas or old behaviors. You create your life from a future perspective, eyes firmly fixed on the person you are becoming, and from a wealth-creation mind-set that looks to future possibilities and opportunities.

You must not be judgmental about your past. If you are judgmental about yourself, you will not be able to take advantage of insights, ideas, and opportunities when you receive them. You must release baggage from the past to prepare to receive what is in store for you in the future.

2. She knows who she is, what she wants—and gives herself permission to be everything she can be (self-awareness).

Our beliefs create our lives. You are who you believe you are. Your world is what you believe it to be. There's a story about two wagon trains arriving in a new town on the western frontier. The first wagon train leader asks an old man sitting on the porch of the general store, "What kind of people will I meet here?" The old man replied with a question, "What kind of people did you meet where you came from?" The new settler thought for a moment, then said, "I met friendly, honest people who worked hard and were always willing to help a neighbor in need." The old man nodded. "That's who you'll meet here." The wagon train leader smiled, thanked the old man, and continued on his way.

A few weeks later, another wagon train arrived and another new settler asked the same question of the old man.

Again, he responded, "What kind of people did you meet where you came from?"

"Mean, lazy, no-counts," he said. "They only thought of themselves and did nothing to help anyone. That's why I left the place."

The old man nodded. "That's who you'll meet here." The wagon train leader grunted and continued on his way.

By their responses to the old man's question, those wagon train leaders said a great deal about themselves and their perceptions of the world. Like them, our attitudes and actions are shaped by our perceptions of the world. Those perceptions also shape people's reactions to us. It reminds me of the old saying, "Wherever you go, there you are."

When you see yourself as weak, incapable, powerless, and poor, others will see you that way. When you see yourself accomplishing nothing, you will do nothing.

When you perceive yourself as strong, able, empowered, and a wealth creator, others see you that way. When you see yourself accomplishing something, you will do something. You enable yourself to reach and live your potential and your dreams.

Vanessa Williams made history as the first Black Miss America. A few weeks later, she made history as the first dethroned beauty queen. The *Penthouse* scandal would have crippled a woman who did not have Vanessa's vision of herself and what she wanted to achieve. She wanted to be a singer, a Broadway performer. She always saw herself on stage. Overcoming the controversy and the critics, she is now living her dreams, and her talents can be enjoyed in movies, at concerts, on TV, on CDs, and on stage.

You must know what it would take for you to become a more effective person. You must become knowledgeable about your hopes, preferences, and desires.

What is your heart's desire? What are you willing to stand for?

3. She has simple requirements for her life: quality and excellence (quality).

You must be committed to giving and receiving only the best. This means doing your best at what you do best.

It means finding a livelihood or wealth-creation vehicle that matches your authentic skills, abilities, and talents. It means being around people who believe the same thing. Creating quality networks where you can share your abilities with others, as well as benefit from others' experiences, can enhance the quality of your wealth-creation journey.

4. She perceives her world as filled with joy and abundance (possibility thinking).

Give yourself permission to experience happiness and prosperity, and encourage others to do the same.

To live with a poverty mind-set means acting as though there is never enough in life. This outlook can become a self-fulfilling prophecy. A prosperity mind-set brings enough for yourself and everyone around you.

By operating out of an abundance mind-set, you are willing to give, share, and receive. A possibility attitude can influence people around you, whether family or the loan officer at the bank. Belief in abundance will allow you to pursue your dreams wholeheartedly and not hold back because you believe there won't be enough for you or anyone else.

5. She finds that independence is within herself (interdependence).

You no longer need to wait for security, freedom, or approval when you find that your independence lives within you. Being able to rely on yourself is the ultimate freedom. This doesn't mean that you live in a vacuum and never seek help from others or provide assistance. In fact, strength and independence are not compromised by reaching out to others to get or give support.

Trusting in your dreams and abilities frees you to make full use of your creative ideas and to follow your goals. Believe you cannot fail, but only choose not to go further on a particular path. Trusting in yourself allows you to know when to change directions and when to move on.

6. She has the energy and excitement to go after her desires (energy).

Vitality will help you to create money and will provide you with the financial support to continue your journey.

Diligence and perseverance will be rewarded. I know a woman named Lee who, from the time she was a little girl, wanted to be a successful businesswoman.

As a girl, she kept a scrapbook of pictures that she cut out of magazines. The pictures represented aspects of life that Lee wanted when she grew up. Unknowingly, Lee sought out role models. An avid reader, she was always interested in reading success stories about women. She recorded the attributes of successful women in her scrapbooks and later in her journals.

Because of her interest in money, Lee decided she wanted to be in banking. The banks, she reasoned, kept all the money. She even used to pretend she was a banker like the few women bankers she saw on television.

Lee is now an investment banker with her own firm

in Atlanta. She does investment banking and bond deals with major corporations and pension funds. She said she believes she ultimately attained this position because she consistently visualized her dreams, believed in herself, and worked very consistently for many, many years to accomplish her goal.

7. She deliberately chooses to focus on the possibilities and opportunities around her (vision).

A Sister *cashing in* avoids getting sucked into the vicious cycle that keeps her spending and in debt.

When you are bored and frustrated by the job and work you do all day, you miss opportunities. You transfer your boredom to everything you see, and it puts more distance between you and the fulfillment of your dreams.

By creating a vision of what you want to be, do, and have, you focus yourself and your energies on the possibilities for your future. Your vision of success will help you see the opportunities that can make you successful. A compelling vision helps pave the road to reach your goals and dreams.

A consistent plan for your life, lifestyle, and livelihood is necessary, as is taking personal responsibility for paying the price for your success. You should be well aware of your personal pattern for success and develop your own blueprints and strategic plans that are consistent with your values and beliefs.

8. She readily accepts the flow of life (adaptability).

You need to be able to adapt to unforeseen challenges and to see problems as opportunities for growth. This requires the belief that you have the confidence and skills to "figure it out." Instead of being crippled by fear, you can be empowered by your faith. You need to develop the ability to let go of what is not working and move to the next opportunity. Life is always full of new opportunities, and paying attention to what is going on around you prepares you to be ready, willing, and able when an opportunity arises—even when it comes disguised as a problem or a setback.

ARE YOU A SISTER?

Assess where you stand with the traits of a Sister *cashing in*. Get eight sheets of paper (or use your notebook or journal). At the top of each sheet, write one of the eight general traits of the enterprising woman: forgiveness, self-awareness, quality, possibility thinking, interdependence, energy, vision, and adaptability.

On each sheet, make two columns. Write "Strengths" at the top of column 1 and "Weaknesses" at the top of column 2. Write at least two things under each column for each trait. Be honest. You don't have to show it to anyone but yourself.

You will see areas where you are strong and some where you need improvement. That's fine. You can set mini goals or daily actions to help bridge the gap between where you are and where you want to be. You may want to look into books or courses on self-improvement or self-awareness. Improving your diet and exercise routine might help with vitality. Even a small decision about your daily activities can take you on the road to independence. Remember, small steps are important as you begin this journey. Save the eight pages so that you can refer to them as you build your wealth-creation skills.

As you look at the requirements of the enterprising woman, remember that they point to the resolve and determination you need to build wealth. Building wealth is a journey and a process that takes time and effort. Now you are ready to look at the changes or improvements you will need to make to create the new possibilities you desire for your life. Find Sisters who have already achieved what you desire. Look at the difference between your behavior and their behavior. Model the behavior that is consistent with you making your financial dreams come true based on your beliefs and values.

❦

Chapter Seven

Taking the LEAP: Love, Energy, Authenticity, and Purpose

Y OU may begin to dream of a better future for yourself by asking, "What are successful people doing that I'm not doing?" "What could I achieve if I started incorporating some of their behaviors into my life?"

The answer is to use the traits of the *cashing-in* Sister to break free from the weight of past habits, mistakes, pains, and other issues that keep you on the money-go-round or locked in other self-defeating behaviors. You cannot start *cashing in* until you form a better relationship with yourself first and with money second.

In working with women over the years, I have developed a way to apply four key principles to your life that can most effectively guide you on your wealth-creation journey. Those principles are love, energy, authenticity, and purpose. The first letters of these principles form the acronym LEAP, which is appropriate because taking the LEAP helps you get off the money-go-round.

Catherine made the choice to take the LEAP after she ran into Monique, an old high school friend. She worked as a receptionist at a major law firm and she made extra income by selling Mary Kay cosmetics. Monique appeared happy, looked good, and had a new boyfriend. She was enthusiastic about the extra money she was making. She talked about the successful people she was meeting and how excited she was about her future income potential.

Looking at Monique, Catherine wondered where she had gone wrong. She was riding the money-go-round and never had enough money. Catherine was surprised at Monique's success because she had been smarter than Monique in high school. She felt that if Monique could be successful, anybody could.

When Monique invited her to a Mary Kay meeting, Catherine readily agreed. At the meeting, she saw other people from her past. They were like Monique: happy, energetic, optimistic. Catherine noticed that her old friends had a different attitude about themselves and money than she did. They were talking about making money, lots of it, and they believed they could do it because in fact many of them *were* doing it.

Her encounter with Monique helped open Catherine's eyes. She looked around and began to see that not everyone was living in the same conditions as she was, even people who earned the same income. They lived better because they spent and invested their time, energy, and money differently. She came to realize that many people were making money differently, and that some people actually enjoyed their work! Some were doing what they loved for a living with an energy she lacked in her job.

With this realization, Catherine started to consider the possibility that she, too, could become happy and successful. She began to think about not just getting rich but building wealth for herself and her family. She was ready to begin her wealth-creation journey and start *cashing in*.

LEAP INTO WEALTH CREATION

Taking the LEAP is the bridge you cross to make the transition from trying to get rich to actually creating wealth. Following are the four principles that will make that transition possible.

Love

Love means learning to love yourself, to love others, and to love your life in general.

Loving yourself helps you let go of the emotional baggage and regrets you carry around with you. Instead of feeling inadequate, give yourself credit for what you have accomplished. Stop withholding approval from yourself. Appreciate yourself first. Be gentle, considerate, forgiving, respectful, responsible, friendly, and courteous to yourself. Loving yourself also includes being understanding, compassionate, fair, ethical, and accountable. You must learn to love yourself unconditionally, whether you have money or not. This will help you forgive yourself if you make a mistake, and to have the confidence to forge ahead when problems arise. When you learn to love yourself that way, you can love others in the same fashion.

Gratitude is an aspect of love. Many people shared with me that they were poor when they were growing up, but they weren't aware of the extent of their poverty because there was so much love in their homes and in their extended families. It seems as though love really helped those families feel secure, because they were grateful for their blessings. Indeed, love made a difference to their ability to survive.

Compassion goes with love. You have to love, support, and nuture yourself just the way you are. Until you feel more love for yourself, you will not be capable of allowing others to be generous to you.

Fear is the opposite of love. Often we act or do not act out of fear. Actions taken out of fear are not necessarily the best choices. So, you need to make the shift from fear to love, which will enable you to make positive changes by being honest with yourself and loving yourself responsibly and unconditionally.

Energy

Energy is a dynamic quality. Energy is a power like electricity or heat that we get from different sources and in many forms. Love is energy. So is personal mastery. Spirituality is energy. Money is another source of energy. Self-acceptance creates energy. There are others as well. You have to recognize what provides you with power and what energy you give off that creates power for others, including your family, your business, and your community.

Because you need energy to move toward your goals, make sure you know how to keep a good supply of it in your life. If you draw energy from your spirit, then know what you need to do to keep your flame lit. Spend time alone or attend a church, study group, or a networking meeting. Your energy level can be jump-started in many ways. Generally, you gain energy when you are utilizing your God-given skills, talents and abilities. The thought of creating a new future for yourself will also bring you new energy. You need to harness your energy and become the author or producer of your own future. Developing the script for your own life can raise your energy level and propel you to action. When you have made the commitment that you want to cash in, you will gain new sources of energy. You will be excited about getting up in the morning. You will be excited about what's next in your life. To harness the creative energy necessary to manifest your inner needs in your life, you have to acknowledge them.

Attend to the talents within you. By attending to those talents you can be fully engaged in your work and in your life. When you are fully engaged, you can convert that positive energy into wealth.

Authenticity

Authenticity means having integrity with your true values and desires. It means be yourself, be true to yourself.

It is unnatural to try to be something other than yourself. You will have freedom and personal power when you choose to be authentic. People can see right through you when you are trying to be someone other than yourself, and it is hard work that wastes your energy. Authenticity is about being genuine, and defines the truth in an individual. It is the expression of security about who you are, what you believe, and what you want your life to mean. Authenticity also creates more and more energy and power. As we become authentic as human beings, we project a light or powerfulness that others find attractive. Trust and trustworthiness are created from authenticity.

I cannot say that if you are authentic, you will make $50,000 more a year. The reverse could be the case. You might give up $50,000 a year to be authentic. Remember, wealth is not defined by money alone. Achieving authenticity can bring more or less money, but it certainly brings more inner peace, personal power, believability, groundedness, centeredness, harmony, and creativity. Who could put a price on that?

You have the freedom to express yourself fully and freely, and to engage in authentic self-expression. Get centered and be happy with who you are. Once you find your authentic path and follow it, all the other puzzle pieces will start to fall into place: the job, the relationship, and the money.

Purpose

The last component of the LEAP strategy is purpose. Your purpose makes itself known to you by what motivates you, what attracts you, what you attract, what energizes you, what excites you, what absorbs you, and what others admire in you. Knowing your purpose will enable you to develop projects that will further the journey toward realizing your dreams. Purpose is actually the fruit born from activating your energy.

As an adult, you have had numerous work-related or personal experiences, and you know which experiences felt right and which ones didn't. Focus on the experiences that felt right, that left you feeling energized and alive, free and positive. What were they? What made them right? Make a list of three of these experiences. Describe what you did, why you loved doing it, and what you believe you achieved or how you or others benefited.

As you look at the list, you should see that these experiences had things in common. They probably met an internal need or purpose, or involved doing something that you liked to do. You drew upon personal resources or talents, and by expressing them you created power and wealth that remain with you today.

If you are unable to recall three experiences where you felt you had a purpose, think instead of three people you believe know and live their purpose. Describe what you see in them and their actions that made you select them. You may be able to define your purpose by examining theirs.

Purpose and meaning present opportunities to grow into a full human being. When you discover what your purpose is, you will also discover what you need to do to fulfill that purpose. Truly wealthy people use their daily lives to expand their sense of self and to accomplish their purpose. You have to let go of people, places, and circumstances that don't help you serve your purpose. Material and financial reward comes as a result of your appreciation for the things you are doing to fulfill your purpose. Your purpose drives action, which means you must be willing to support your purpose with passion.

It may take time to discover your purpose. Many of us make false starts. Throughout our lives, we can have several different purposes: we may need to achieve one thing before we can achieve another. Joan of Arc knew her purpose at age sixteen and became a military leader in the campaign to restore Charles VII to the French throne. Harriet Tubman found her purpose in the Underground Railroad and pursued it despite rewards for her capture totaling about $40,000, a great fortune in those days. Anna Mary Robertson Moses found her first purpose in being a great farm wife and caring mother to her children and grandchildren. Then, in her seventies, she found another purpose. She picked up a paintbrush, and her colorful, simple scenes of rural life made her famous as Grandma Moses. It is never too early to define or discover your purpose and never too late to choose a new purpose and pursue it. Having a purpose allows you to have a meaningful way of life.

Gaining clarity about your individual purpose is no different from gaining clarity about anything else. You have to connect with your purpose at a feeling level; it isn't a purely intellectual exercise. It's intuitive, too.

Doing what you love and loving what you do is the ultimate vehicle for your livelihood, fulfillment, and financial freedom. Relinquishing what is not right for your life's purpose allows you the freedom and the room to pursue what you love. The daily activities that are meant to be your life's work are the very things that you will love to do with your time and energy. When you sincerely love what you do, you will never feel as if you are working another day in your life, because you will feel so alive, so happy and fulfilled that your work will not seem like work at all.

Doing what you love is a process of self-discovery. You must learn to listen to yourself rather than always seeking answers from others. Be aware of the pitfall of dedicating yourself to another's dreams. Never allow yourself to be discouraged by others who insist that what you are seeking is too difficult or unrealistic to accomplish. Nor should you let anyone else's ideas or opinions about what you should do affect the path you take in life. Only *you* can know what that path is. Doing what you love to do may be something quite different from what others had in mind for you. It may not even be what you have been trained or educated to do. Only *you* know what you truly love. Doing what you love requires that you come to grips with your need, and your aspirations. You have all the power you need to find your right livelihood. It may be buried under layers of rejection or fear, but it's there. You don't have to feel guilty if you want to alter your purpose. Your purpose may expand with greater opportunities for creativity, learning and growing. Product knowledge begins with self-awareness. Career management, like any business, begins with knowing what's in the warehouse—what the product is, what the purpose and passion are. You must begin with knowledge of yourself—your product—before you go to market.

LEAPING TO FREEDOM, WEALTH, AND POWER

The wealth you seek through *cashing in* is more than just money. It is a wealth of abundance and prosperity that enriches us inside and out.

True wealth is having all you need to do your life's work—the tools, resources, living environment—and to live a life full of joy and abundance. It is the intangible things that bring us inner peace. We all know of the rich, famous, successful people who have all of the machinery of the American dream: big houses, new cars, fast boats, expensive jewelry, private jets, their pictures on TV and in the newspaper. Then, every once in a while, we hear about these people checking into a clinic where they can detox; going through multiple, unsuccessful, intimate relationships; or attempting suicide. We know that money by itself does not bring the well-being I am speaking about. I've met people who earn over a quarter of a million dollars but are fearful and feel they never have enough money. These people can't imagine how to take care of themselves without having more things, more status, and more power over others.

I've met people who live on very little money but are self-sufficient, secure, quietly self-contained, and supportive of all living things, especially their children, their community, and their church.

True wealth has little to do with outer trappings, such as material wealth, country club memberships, a steady job, a steady man, a big house, or a little house. It has everything to do with our inner condition, stance, or frame of reference. Ask yourself these questions:

— *What elements of my current lifestyle do I really need?*

— *What elements do I want?*

— *What elements could I do without or economize on?*

I am not saying that true wealth can come only from living a bare-bones existence of shelter, food, and water. True wealth includes having enough. If we do live a basic life, to do so must be a deliberate choice. The motivation for true wealth comes from our authentic purpose and goals, not from being passively victimized by external expectations of us.

True wealth is a way of being and not a way of having or a way of getting something. We each have a personal path, life, or journey to follow. We all have something distinctive about ourselves as individuals. If we listen, we can hear the call. Following that is our surest route to our blessings, our fulfillment, and our inheritance as human beings.

ACTIONS OF AFFIRMATION

Think of one thing that you can improve, change, or do that will enhance your love, energy, authenticity, and purpose. It might be something as simple as pampering yourself with a scented bath for an hour. Such a spa experience can rejuvenate your physical and spiritual energy. If you currently engage in an activity or habit that you need to stop because it violates your health, values or beliefs, consider seeking assistance from a health practitioner, coach, or counselor.

The way to wealth is through inner peace and harmony. The wealth that you want, inner and outer wealth, involves using what you have—your possessions, your God-given gifts and talents—and using them so well that they multiply. Unfortunately, most people are too fearful to use or invest in their own natural possessions and gain total wealth.

The dictionary defines wealth as "an abundance of valuable material possessions or resources." That's not all it is. To achieve the wealth I am speaking of, you have to blend what you have within you, your authenticity, with your external life. When you do, you will begin to have so much that you can give it away.

You don't want to have only material possessions at the end of your life. You don't want to have regrets at the end of your life, wishing you had done this or done that, or wishing you had said this or that. You certainly don't want to end life wishing you had loved more. Seeking only the material part of wealth can keep you away from more important pursuits.

Material gains should add to your personal wealth, not detract from it. It is okay to have the intention to make money, but money is not something worth spending a lifetime worrying about. It is simply a tool to help you expand your self-empowerment. With your beliefs and actions, you are the creator of money and everything else in your life. Place your desire for money in context with your desire for the other things you want your life to have: love, energy, authenticity, and purpose.

When you have determined what you want, take actions to achieve it, but don't always seek instant gratification. You may need to plan and postpone your desires in order to fulfill them.

Setting money aside in a consistent fashion builds savings and can pave the way to achieving wealth. Savings are fluid, accessible, easily redeemable cash. Savings give you resources that allow you to be self-sufficient. You can take advantage of opportunities when you have money saved. Savings give you flexibility and allow you more choices and more freedom. Savings also allow you to have greater control over the timing of purchases. Some things you want may require a large sum of money. By having savings available, you can get what you want when you want it. Don't think of saving only for an emergency or disaster. Envision your savings as a wealth-creation account.

One of the best uses of your savings is to master your authentic skills so you can create your livelihood. People who become wealthy put their extra money into their dreams. They focus on what they love to do, and almost always invest their money in their own work, not in investments they aren't familiar with. Spend money on things that will help you get your authentic self out into the world: books, tapes, coaching classes and seminars, equipment, a computer, a home office.

You can use LEAP to help you put money in its proper perspective. Understanding your relationship with money takes love, energy, and authentic self-expression. You will never be free if you say that you have more than enough money, then act and think as if you don't. You'll never be free if you think you don't have enough money, then act as if you do. Authentic self-expression means you can't be worried about keeping up with the Joneses.

FINDING THE TRUE YOU FROM THE INSIDE OUT

Love, energy, authenticity, and purpose are defining qualities for our internal selves, and are the pieces that must be in place for us to cope effectively with the outside world. They comprise the image we see when we look in the mirror.

On the outside, too many of us look like we have it all together. When people look at us, we are dressed beautifully, are neatly manicured, and we are hanging on the right man's arm or with the right group of connected women. But we cannot always tell by a person's outside appearance whether they have inner stability. A good facial can temporarily give a woman the kind of glow that comes from self-fulfillment. But inner security, that deeper level of enrichment, is something money cannot buy. On the inside, we may live in a state of distress, of anxiety and fearfulness, and yearn for something more in our lives. We fear that we won't make the cut if people know what we earn, save, or own. We fear being found out. We fear people might think different of us if we had the courage to live our dreams.

If we surrender our power to the external world, we won't make the most of our inner resources—intelligence, dreams, hunches, the personal instinct that we have within ourselves all the time.

Your public life should flow out of your private life. Be, do, and have quality. Achieve personal mastery and effectiveness. "Inside out" means to start with self, to start with the most fundamental insides of self. To cultivate your internal wealth, you might try meditation, visualization, and/or prayer. Quiet contemplation may change your perspective of yourself. And how you view yourself has a lot to do with how you view the world around you.

Love, energy, authenticity, and purpose help make it possible to lose the weight of past habits, pains, and other defeating behavior. You can LEAP into the kind of wealth that fills both your soul and your bank accounts.

Chapter Eight

Your Starting Point on the Wealth-Creation Journey

Do you remember the last trip you took? Whether it was across town or across the world, you needed to take certain things with you: a driver's license or passport, appropriate clothes, camera, and so on. You also needed to know your destination and how to get there. You needed a map if you were driving or a bus, train, or plane ticket if you were leaving the transportation to someone else.

You are about to embark on a wealth-creation journey, and this time you are in the driver's seat. You'll be guided by your internal compass. Before you start, you have to know your destination. What do you want to be doing? Where are you going? Where do you want to live? What people do you want in your life? At the end of your journey, who will you be? Where do you want to be? I've met people who were miserable in the freezing winds of the North when they needed the warm soil of their native South. What environment do you need to thrive? Give consideration to these and other aspects of your destination before you determine where you want to go. The journey is uniquely yours, no one else's. So the path has to be your own.

You also must know what you need to pack. Some of the things you pack should help you read road signs and recognize potholes that may stand in your way, and ramps that get you on and off the road. To gauge the length of the trip, you have to know the distance between your starting point and your destination. As with any trip, being prepared makes the journey more fun and guarantees success.

Eliminate the obstacles. Take fear along as your companion, not as your guide. Be prepared to run into potholes along the way. When you question whether the journey will be worth the effort, remember your reasons for taking the journey in the first place—you want your financial dreams to come true.

SELECT YOUR DESTINATION

If you don't know where you're going, you are going to end up where you don't want to be. Pick the destination and then the route to take. If your destination is college, your route is determined by the things you need to take care of in order to get there. Do you need to take the SAT or GRE? Before you take the test, do you need a study skills class to help you get the score your college requires for admission? Do you have the money for tuition, will your company pay or do you need to apply for financial aid? There are other things to consider, too. Draw upon friends, people doing similar things, and other resources so you can plan the best route to your destination.

Do Your Homework

Thanks to the World Wide Web, you can swiftly put together information that will help you achieve your goal. You can determine if there are different "legs" to your journey or different paths you can follow. For example, after law school, you can clerk for a judge, join a major law firm, open your own practice, or become a circuit court judge—be sure to research your options. Read about others who lived a dream like yours so that you can learn from their experiences.

Pick the Best Route for You

Like cars on the freeway, some people need to travel in the fast lane. They step on the gas at seventy miles an hour. For others, it is important to keep the speedometer at fifty-five miles an hour. What works for other people might not work for you. Be honest about your needs and your goals so you can pick the route and travel the way that is best for you.

Pack Carefully

You need your honesty and authenticity on this journey. You will have to be brutally honest with yourself about the progress you are making and about what you need to make progress. Select the tools to get what you want and the measurement to use for checking progress. If your goal is to lose twenty pounds in twelve months, the tools are your exercise and diet. Your measurements might be how you feel, and that your clothes fit better, as well as numbers on the scale. If your goal is to retire at fifty-five, you would need to measure your rate of return on savings and investments, plus the number of years you have before your fifty-fifth birthday, against the level of annual income needed to support you through your retirement years. Be honest about what you want to achieve and the time you want to give yourself to achieve it.

Pack things that will help on the journey, like your unique skills, talents, and good habits. Do not bring the things that have held you back in the past. Leave all your old baggage behind.

Don't be attached to the outcome. You are part of the process, so measure the results honestly. It is possible that the results will not be what you want. For example, a friend of mine participated in a weight loss program. She got frustrated that she lost a pound each week when losing two pounds was her goal. She followed the program faithfully—and faithfully she lost a pound a week. Although this was not the result she wanted, the process yielded the results it could under the circumstances. To ease her frustration, she modified her goals to match the results she was getting and reevaluated her ultimate goal. It did take her longer to lose the weight, but she did eventually lose the weight—which was her desired outcome in the first place.

Determine a Mini-Goal for Every Hundred Miles Traveled

You will need rewards along your journey to keep you motivated and on track. Establish performance points so that you can see you are making progress toward your goal. For example, you could forgive yourself for a mistake you made years ago, attend a seminar that makes you computer-proficient (not just computer-literate), or cut up and pay off a credit card.

Move Through Your Journey with Your Purpose in Mind

Keeping your goal in mind will help keep you focused and will keep you from being sidetracked. There is a difference between being sidetracked and taking a detour. Getting sidetracked takes you off your chosen path. It's like starting to Thanksgiving dinner at your mother's and stopping at the mall and staying so long, you miss the meal! Often, taking a detour is necessary. If you decide to start a business, but the building you want to buy to house your business requires two years of remodeling, you might detour to rental space. If your dream of the future requires you to have skills that you don't have right now, take the detour to night classes at the local community college or a weekend seminar to get the skills, then continue on your route. With information technology changing rapidly, you may have to detour from your plans to learn about something that does not even exist today! Don't panic if you occasionally need to make a detour.

Concentrating on your purpose keeps you focused on traveling to your goal. However, focus does not make you blind or indifferent to others on the road. Wealth creation doesn't require trampling people underfoot or knocking them aside. You do have to navigate, though. Keep your eyes fixed on your goal and walk with purpose. Some people will assist you and share your journey. Other people will get in your way. When you see they cannot help you or when you see they will only hinder you, move around them.

Keep a Realistic Calendar or Journal

While you are on your journey, keep a calendar or journal handy. Give yourself as much time as you need for achieving the goal. You cannot achieve wealth or move to the next level of wealth overnight. Figure out the time stages you need. (They are those points marked "by when," as in *I need to order my passport by January to have it in time for my trip to Argentina at Easter* or *I need to lease the building by September to open by mid-November*.) Plot them on your calendar. Write in pencil, not ink, so that you can make adjustments if necessary. Write about your journey in the journal. It will help you keep track of your accomplishments and can serve as a boost when you are feeling stuck at some point on your journey.

STAY FIT

Poor health not only will slow you down; it also can delay your dreams. You must be healthy and fit to get where you want to go, and to enjoy both the journey and the destination. Plan for regular exercise and healthy eating habits. If your journey needs a detour to a smoking cessation program, or to get weight loss or other health advice, fit it in.

TRAVEL LIGHT

You packed what you needed and considered the detours you needed to make, so be wary of picking up unnecessary items along the way. If a relationship turns sour during your journey, don't bury the pain inside of you, where it will weigh you down. Deal with it in an open and honest manner that will help you get through the trauma without jeopardizing your journey.

Be wary of picking up expensive trappings when your journey proves successful but before you fully achieve your dream. Expensive trappings require a lot of babysitting. For example, women with fur coats worry about handing them over at the coat check and often circulate with the fur draped over their arm or over the arm of their escort. Such trappings boost your insurance bill, too. Be wary of material things that slow you down.

Sometimes, people slow us down. A client of mine had

a brother who got into drugs, and her life was soon consumed by trying to save him. She missed career opportunities because she had to leave work to deal with emergencies, like bailing him out of jail or taking him to a drug treatment program. She often spent the hours from the time she got home until she needed to go to bed looking for him on street corners and in alleys. The brother, a heroin addict, did not appreciate her efforts. He was often verbally and sometimes physically abusive to her. He stole her money from every hiding place she could think of. After a while, she became dispirited, bone-weary, and physically ill. She finally had to accept that what she was doing was not helping her brother or herself. She loved her brother, but saw she could not help him until he was ready to help himself. She refocused on her goals and got back to living a meaningful life of her own.

TRAVELING SOLO OR WITH COMPANIONS

Creating wealth is not necessarily a solitary journey. You can bring your family with you. Children, especially, can learn from your journey so that they can create wealth for themselves in the future. At some points, you may travel alone; at other times, you will be traveling with others. You may need to form alliances or build partnerships to help you through your journey. Because the wealth creation stressed here is designed to help you, your family, and your community, you might want to bring company on your trip.

Watch the Road Signs for Opportunity

There will be many opportunities on your journey, like starting your own business, turning your hobby into your full-time occupation, or learning something about yourself that you never knew before.

Be open to opportunities that you never thought possible. For example, there has been a craze in the last few years over Beanie Babies. A Beanie Baby is a soft, plush toy that has great value as a collectible item if the original tag is in good condition. Well, an enterprising guy invented a plastic doodad to cover the tag—and became a multimillionaire when his product hit the market. He took successful advantage of an opportunity. Other opportunities might lead to loans for your business. Often, financial institutions boost their small business and minority lending in order to win federal approval of bank mergers. Did you know that the U.S. Department of Agriculture offers small business loans when you use farm produce in your products? Reading newspapers and magazines can keep you on top of current events and other news that might inspire ideas. Joining an investment club will give you interaction with people willing to share their knowledge and experience. Keep your eyes open so that you can see the opportunities around you.

Avoid Potholes and Wrong Exits

Be mindful of the habits that kept you on the money-go-round or made you engage in other destructive behavior. Trace the triggers that send you back into those behaviors, and don't let them trip you up again.

STRATEGIC PLANNING FOR YOUR SELF

The wealth-creation journey begins by looking at the roles you play: person, woman, sister, friend, girlfriend, wife, lover, mother, daughter, church member, voter, entrepreneur, worker, and so on.

No matter how you define yourself or the roles you play, freedom, wealth, and power mean change. I remember saying this to a group of business managers and owners in 1995. We had gathered at a conference with the theme "Transforming the Soul of Business," and I had challenged them in my presentation to transform their own souls by mapping out their personal strategic plans before making changes in their businesses. The audience almost gave a collective frown when they heard this. Even at a conference about the *soul* of business, the concept of a personal strategic plan sounded too hokey for them.

These were high-powered businesspeople who would not step into their executive offices without a strategic plan or an operations plan for their business in place. Most of us would never do that. Yet, most of us step in and out of our homes daily without a strategic plan for our lives.

It's not hard to figure out why. When we do business or operations plans, we have to look at the bare bones of the business. Nothing goes unexamined. Nothing is immune from scrutiny—not when our business survival (jobs, competitive edge, revenue)—depends upon it. We have to know our business inside out to effectively make positive changes and enhance our business performance.

In our personal lives, though, most of us avoid such bare-bones self-examination. We hide things from ourselves. We do not examine behaviors that point to patterns. We don't scrutinize how we spend our resources—time, money, and energy.

When I asked the executives at the conference if they would hide inventory or turn a blind eye to consumer buying trends in their businesses, they replied, "Of course not!" They then began to realize the importance of a personal strategic plan.

Remember, like any trip, the wealth-creation journey takes preparation, including a strategic plan for yourself. It is important to know where you want to end your journey before you take off. Make sure you have all the items you need for the journey or be prepared to take detours or form alliances to help you get those items. Anticipate the road signs that will let you know you are on the right track. Recognize that sometimes you will be a Good Samaritan on this journey, and other times another Sister will be a Good Samaritan to you.

Chapter Nine

Chapter Nine

Seeing: The Truth Shall Set You Free

SEEING is the first S on the journey to freedom, wealth, and power. On this journey, you will be asked to engage in reflection, introspection, aspiration, transformation, and action. Seeing is a process of examining your life as it is now and making an assessment of what you have generated for yourself. It is not looking at what was or what could be. I'm not talking about changing things to the way they were in the past, but transforming things to the way you want them to be now and in the future. Are you really being, doing, and having it all?

By becoming aware of where you are, you can begin to take action to get you where you want to be. Not knowing keeps you immobile. Not knowing makes you create inappropriate dreams for yourself. And though the present may not be perfect, it is a place from which to learn, grow, and evolve if you're willing to remain positive, open, and without judgment of yourself and others.

First, let's look at three areas that shape your current situation: your life, your lifestyle, and your livelihood. Your life is based on the inner you. Your lifestyle is based on the external you. Your livelihood is based on your resources. To cash in, your goal is to create a fulfilling lifestyle that is free from debt, fear, and worry and that allows you to create your livelihood by using your God-given skills, talents and abilities.

LIFE, LIFESTYLE, LIVELIHOOD

Are you working for a lifestyle or are you living your life? How much of your life is being consumed by your lifestyle? There is nothing wrong with living a grand lifestyle, but let's make sure you control the lifestyle and the lifestyle doesn't control you. The following twenty-five questions are designed to give you an overview of where you are now and to help you discover elements of your lifestyle. There are no right or wrong answers. Honest answers will give you a true assessment of where you stand. Seeing means observing, but not judging, your present situation. You can think about these questions or write about them in your journal.

QUESTION	YES	NO
1. Do you have the freedom to make the decisions that will give you the lifestyle you desire?		
2. Are you earning your income in a way that is fulfilling?		
3. Are you earning your income in a way that is helping you to grow?		
4. Are you financially prepared to start that business you've been thinking about starting?		
5. Are you preparing for the future?		
6. Are you balancing your checkbook every month?		
7. Do you have adequate insurance coverage for yourself, your loved ones, and your possessions?		
8. Do you have a will or revocable living trust?		
9. Are you carrying high balances on your credit cards?		
10. Are you paying reasonable interest rates?		
11. Are you due for needed medical, dental, or eye exams?		
12. Is your car maintenance up to date?		
13. Do you have unpaid traffic tickets?		
14. Are all of your taxes (income, property, etc.) paid up?		
15. Are your financial records accessible and in order?		

QUESTION	YES	NO
16. If you bill for your services, is your billing up to date?		
17. Do you have a structure for getting bills out on schedule?		
18. Are you giving your children their allowances on a consistent basis?		
19. Do you prepare and follow a monthly budget?		
20. Have you established a mutually acceptable schedule for the repayment of any overdue debts?		
21. Are you paying your student loans off as agreed?		
22. Do you have a retirement plan?		
23. Are you saving money on a consistent basis?		
24. Are you sharing your money on a consistent basis?		
25. Do you have a financial expert coaching or advising you?		

SPENDING FOR LIFE

Most Sisters, regardless of our economic condition, are paying too much for what we are getting out of life. We spend our time chasing a lifestyle when we could be living. No matter how much we make, we spend that and just a little bit more. It is hard for most of us to admit to ourselves that we have been seduced by our lifestyles. We haven't accepted the equation that less lifestyle (trappings, money-go-round pursuits, and so on) equals more life (freedom, wealth, and power). Most of us are trapped by our lifestyles. We're living paycheck to paycheck, supporting lifestyles that are too expensive, rather than saving and investing our money. Many of us are living lifestyles of the rich and famous, but we're living so close to the edge that we can't afford to progress in meaningful and fulfilling ways. We are forced to keep working the jobs we have instead of discovering meaningful work that is more aligned with our God-given skills, gifts, and talents. As long as we feel forced to fund our lifestyles, we cannot afford to stop working, start a business, or engage in other creative ventures. We are not creating freedom, wealth, and power. But we do have the choice to simplify our lifestyle. Choosing a life over a lifestyle requires becoming more instead of having more.

DETERMINE YOUR NET WORTH

Without knowing what your financial condition is, it will be impossible for you to determine areas that need improvement and establish a plan of action to heal your relationship with money. That is why knowing your net worth is significant in creating your future and your lifestyle. Net worth is roughly the value of your assets if you paid all your debts now. You want to have a positive net worth, which means that the value of what you own is more than the amount of what you owe. Make a list of the things you own and their current value. (Remember that the value of things can increase or decrease. You can use the *Blue Book* to determine your car's value. If you own your home, use your property assessment or check the real estate listings for selling prices on similar homes in your neighborhood.) Next, make a list of what you owe. Subtract what you owe from the value of what you own. The amount left is your net worth.

If your net worth is not where it should be, there are four ways to increase your net worth: 1) clear up debt, 2) spend less, 3) invest, 4) earn more money.

COMPLETE INCOMPLETE BUSINESS

Look at the roles and dramas you choose to take on. We may know we can't afford it, but nevertheless we run up large debts and borrow heavily against our houses and our incomes.

A closer look at our own finances often reveals that we have co-signed unwise loans rather than admit that what we're really longing for is acceptance, acknowledgment, and love. We're human; we all want love and acceptance. We have used money to manipulate our relationships. We have hidden it, lied about it, and become vague rather than admit we give access to our money to others because we don't want to risk the loss of their love and acceptance. We have ruined our credit ratings, used our savings, denied our dreams in order to finance the shaky schemes of our loved ones or people we want to love us. We place our own feelings and meanings on the words and actions of those we care for. In the process, we feel sad, mad, hurt, unloved, and unappreciated. We lose our feelings of self-worth, self-respect, and self-esteem. Then we become distrustful, fearful, and cynical. These thoughts and feelings influence our attitudes and behaviors and become our core issues; we carry them into other areas of our lives. These core issues have such huge amounts of energy locked up in them that until we are willing to free this energy, we will experience increasing stress and discomfort. Our core issues not only affect us, they affect everyone with whom we live, work, and interact. And although it takes a great deal of focused attention, commitment, and perseverance to open the energy around those core issues, until we are willing to do so, we deny ourselves the gift of knowing what a full life, full of expression of self, feels like, and how powerful we really are. When we do free these energies, we will notice an increase in our personal power.

Often we leave our money business unfinished because of broader unresolved issues. For instance, you may be feeling insecure or embarrassed about money because you're in debt and you're struggling to make ends meet. Each time you neglect to handle your finances in a responsible way, you may be sending yourself that old message of not being good enough, not being worthy, and so on. By ignoring the issue, you let denial and inaction catch up with you through more debt, blemished credit reports, and embarrassment. Using the tool of seeing is like becoming conscious, like moving from the darkness into the light. You cannot change what you do not know and acknowledge. Get an accurate account of your income and expenses, and determine where your money goes each week. Pay your bills on time.

GIVE UP THE STRUGGLE

Life was not meant to be a struggle. If your attitude is positive or proactive, you will probably manage your money better than if it is negative or reactive. Many Sisters avoid dealing with money issues until there is a crisis. They don't pay their bills until the late notices come in the mail. They recognize a shut-off notice from a utility because it usually comes in a colored envelope. They neglect to balance their checkbooks until they receive overdraft notices. They spend all of their money and don't make savings a priority until they hit middle age and begin to realize that their past behaviors are going to harm their present and their future. Responsibly handling your finances can help end your struggle.

BE HONEST WITH YOURSELF

Get real with yourself about your life. Be truthful about what isn't working. If you lie to yourself about any dimension of your life, you can distort the entire picture so much that an otherwise sound strategy will be compromised. There are two ways that people usually lie to themselves: failing to say what is, and misrepresenting what is. You have to have the strength and courage to ask yourself the hard questions and give yourself realistic answers.

You have to be willing to allow every belief, every position, every pattern in your life to be questioned, examined, and challenged. You have to be willing to assess your beliefs, positions, and patterns honestly. You cannot afford the luxury of defensiveness, lies, and denial. Each delays or destroys dreams and possibilities.

You have to be willing to admit to yourself that you feel lost, scared, hopeless, or alienated. Believe that your life is not too damaged to be repaired and it's not too late to fix it. But be honest about what needs fixing. Being honest means taking off the rose-colored glasses and seeing the world and your life clearly. What's going on in your life that may be threatening your hopes and dreams for the future? Maybe the truth you must embrace pertains to others in your life, but maybe the truth has to do with you. If your life, lifestyle, or livelihood situation is not the way you want it to be, admit it. If you're bitter, hostile, jealous, or angry, admit it. If you're scared, admit it. Be honest, because you may be cheating yourself out of the best chance you've ever had to really cash in and live the life of your dreams and heart's desire: being, doing, and having all you want. Learn from your current life to get and give what you really want.

BE WILLING TO TAKE RESPONSIBILITY FOR YOUR LIFE

If you are unable or unwilling to identify and consciously acknowledge the behaviors, characteristics, or life patterns that are not supporting you, then you will not change them. I want you to acknowledge whatever is not working in your life right now that has an effect upon the overall well-being of your life, lifestyle, and livelihood. That could include self, relationships, career, environment, and so on. If it's not working, you have three choices: accept it, live with it, or change it. I am inviting you to determine which you can do. But, first you have to see or be honest with yourselves to determine what "it" is.

Acknowledgment is a no-kidding, unvarnished, bottom-line confrontation with yourself about what you are doing or not doing, or what you are putting up with in your life that is not contributing to creating the future you want for yourself. It's authentic. It's no hocus-pocus or politically correct answer. Know that it is okay to dream. Freedom comes when we are true to ourselves. When we don't have freedom, we know it is missing. Take a look at the life you have created for yourself and own it. Is this the life you want for yourself and your future?

CONSIDER THE TRADE-OFFS

Knowing what you need to do, how to do it, and why you do it are very different things. Why do you behave in ways that generate results that you do not want and that keep you from getting the results you do want? You have to start behaving in ways consistent with producing the results you want in your life. For example, if you are committed to being healthy, you will no longer delay getting a prescription filled at the pharmacy or making an appointment for a health checkup. However, usually you maintain nonproductive behavior because you are making some kind of a trade-off; otherwise, you wouldn't do it. It's like being on a diet and eating a piece of chocolate cake. You know eating it is not consistent with your weight loss goal, but you eat the cake anyway because the trade-off is the delicious taste and not being dominated by the diet.

If your behavior didn't serve some sort of purpose, or generate some value, you wouldn't do it. This concept of trade-off is important in shaping all sorts of behavior. But you may not realize what you perceive to be a reward. You cannot eliminate unwanted behavior without understanding why you do it to begin with. Only then will you know what buttons to push to get the desired change in your own behavior or that of others. The challenge is to consider all the possible ways you could be trading a long-term goal for a short-term gain.

Is money your motivator? Monetary trade-offs may be the primary reason you go to work every day rather than make a livelihood by doing something you love. Do you value money so much that you are willing to make certain sacrifices, to do certain things, in order to get it?

Are you looking for love? Psychological income can take the form of acceptance, approval, praise, love, companionship, greed, punishment, or fulfillment—as well as feelings of safety and security. These trade-offs act powerfully to condition you to repeat the behaviors that bring them about.

Are you so spiritual that you are no earthly good? Spiritual income is a trade-off that can manifest itself in terms of peace, sense of connection to a higher power, or feeling of righteousness and morality. But it may keep you from living in the real world.

Is looking good or feeling good your priority? Physical income is the often-powerful sense of physical well-being that comes from good nutrition, exercise, proper weight management, and healthy lifestyle.

Is making a difference your driving force? Achievement income is a feeling of accomplishment; recognition from others within one's field of endeavor; or an inner awareness of a job well done. But if you give away too much of yourself, there won't be anything left for you.

Is being part of a team what makes you tick? Social income derives from feeling that you are part of a group and increases when you feel you not only belong but are a contributor or leader. There is nothing wrong with being a team player, but if it holds you back from your own dreams and goals, it might be time to go solo.

All of these categories of trade-offs are at work in every Sister's life. You may be money-driven, or you may be more motivated by achievement, but make no mistake, the behaviors that you exhibit regularly are influenced and maintained by these various types of income. As you seek to understand why you act in certain ways, look hard and honestly at what you are getting out of what you are doing. Ask yourself, "What am I getting out of this? What's my trade-off?" In some cases the trade-off will be obvious; in other cases you'll have to do some digging. Are you working so hard for achievement income that you avoid family commitments? Or are you so dominated by family trade-offs that you fail to meet your livelihood and other financial needs? Focusing on any one aspect of your life can keep you from achieving in the others.

You may engage in these behaviors because you are avoiding responsibility. Sometimes it's easier to let things stay the same, as unpleasant as they may be, rather than venture out and try something new. Most Sisters want to be accepted and fear rejection. We can live out of love or out of fear. Fear may be so strong that you are willing to do almost anything to avoid it.

You may also want to consider immediate versus delayed gratification. Our demand for immediate gratification creates an appetite for a small trade-off now rather than *cashing in* later. This may explain why you spend money now instead of saving for the future. You might say, *It will be nice to have money twenty or thirty years from now, but I want this expensive dress today.* Just remember, when you choose the behavior, you choose the consequences.

You might want to consider that your trade-off has something to do with taking a risk because you want to make yourself right and someone else wrong. Become aware of the persistent complaints that you make. Persistent complaints allow you to be right. For example, many people complain that they have "too much to do" and "can't possibly get it all done." This persistent complaint gives you a trade-off of shifting the responsibility for taking on additional projects. It may also be an excuse for you not to complete all the tasks you promise to do. Then you have an opportunity to make your boss wrong by saying he or she gave you too many tasks. The complaints might just represent a story that you keep telling yourself. Then you begin to act under the mistaken notion that these complaints represent reality. By examining how your behaviors result in some form of trade-off, you will see what actions need to change in order to get a "positive" trade-off.

Find and manage the trade-offs, and you manage the behavior. When you understand and embrace this concept, your effectiveness will increase dramatically.

Though you are getting trade-offs for your behavior, the costs may prove to be much greater than the trade-offs. They may be the loss of love or of connection with others, loss of health and vitality, lack of fulfillment and satisfaction, lack of self-expression, or delayed effectiveness and productivity.

PICK THE RIGHT FRIENDS

Friends can be allies or can hold you back. Your friends may be people who are willing to agree with your persistent complaints. They don't do that for free. What do you pay them back with? You agree with their complaints. You develop a common bond that says, *You commiserate with me and I'll commiserate with you.* You have pity party after pity party, which keeps you stuck right where you are. Real friends are not energy drainers; they don't take your joy. Pick friends who will allow you to be more powerful than you are and encourage you to be yourself and the best that you can be. Also, be that kind of friend to them.

THE TRUTH WILL SET YOU FREE

Once you acknowledge something is not working and accept ownership for its not working, living in the status quo becomes much more difficult. You take responsibility, and you cannot hide behind other people.

You have to be honest with yourself. Honesty means the truth, the whole truth, and nothing but the truth. No lies. No excuses. It takes courage and commitment to be genuinely honest with yourself.

If you are making promises to yourself that you never keep, admit it. If you have no goals and are going through the motions, day after day, admit it. You must acknowledge that whatever your circumstance is, you created it, you own it.

You can no longer afford to be a spectator in the stands, looking at your life. You have to get out on the court and not only play, but play to win. You have to be committed and focused. You have to stop doing the things that are preventing you from overcoming your obstacles. You have to get in control of creating the future you desire.

What Are You Postponing or Putting Off?

To become aware of what you are postponing or putting off, all you need to do is look at the results you are producing. We always project outside of us a precise picture of what is going on inside of us. You may be postponing or putting off taking responsibility for organizing or planning. Your business affairs are a distinct reflection of who you are. If you are sloppy, your business affairs will be sloppy. If you are disorganized, your business affairs will be disorganized. Consider the cost of what you are postponing or putting off. Postponing or putting off organization and good planning may be losing you money, energy, love, and affection.

It is all right to have money. You may feel guilty about having money, especially when you see others—perhaps your family, extended family, or others in your community—struggling to make ends meet. Some Sisters may say the lack of money is the only reason they are not living the life of their dreams. Will you consider that money is not the real reason? Get rid of all of your reasons, excuses, and convoluted schemes, and look at the conditions in your life as they really are. Be absolutely honest with yourself and critically examine your life, then get a handle on what, in fact, your life *could* be. Acknowledge that there are things about yourself that you can improve, and when those things are improved, your life will be richer and more fulfilling. Take control of your circumstances instead of letting your circumstances control you.

Master the Challenges

Every Sister needs to confront and master the challenges that are holding her back, whether those challenges are the private demons of abusive relationships, the public hurdles built by racism and sexism, a lack of skills that match twenty-first-century business needs, or a naive view of financial management. You can overcome these challenges by tapping the potential, power, and possibilities inside you and your community, so you can take advantage of opportuities ahead. You must lay down your baggage, break through the barriers, and declare you are committed to being the best you can be in all areas of your life.

You can change things for yourself. Remember what your dreams are. What is going on in your life to support your dreams? What is next for you? What's stopping you from making your dreams happen right now? Is something in your way? Is someone? Is that someone you?

You can make your financial dreams come true, no matter what your circumstances, no matter where in the world you are, no matter what your age. It is never too late to begin. It is never too late to begin *again*. Any Sister who ever doubted should doubt no longer with examples such as Madame C. J. Walker, Oprah Winfrey, and Oseola McCarty to learn from. They, and less-known women, chose their mission and marched to the sound of their own drummer. They took advantage of personal and business opportunities, even when it required risks and sacrifices.

You can, too. You can move to the next level in your life and keep moving to higher levels to achieve your dreams, aspirations, and goals. But you have to take personal responsibility. No one else can do this for you. It is important to take the steps to turn your interest into the commitment to yourself and your future. You need to make the commitment to assume total ownership of the part you are going to play in this process. You must believe that the rewards are greater than the price you have to pay. Either you pay now or you pay later, with interest and penalty, by not having the future you want. The information and insights you gain here can help you to pursue your financial goals and aspirations in a meaningful way only when you put them to use. Once you've made the commitment, you will start to see things in a different light, and to see yourself acting differently than you have in the past. You, and only you, play the most important part in *cashing in*.

❦

Chapter Ten

Surrendering: Let Go and Let God

SURRENDERING is a process of becoming empty in order to be made full, to dismantle old habits and self-images in order to be born again.

One of the worst things to emerge as part of the influx of women into the workplace was the concept of *Superwoman*. In the early 1970s, it became the descriptive title for a woman who did it all. Not only did she put in a full day at the office, she also kept house, raised children, and satisfied her man. She could bake cookies, change a flat tire, and give a presentation on projected quarterly earnings.

The Superwoman concept was unrealistic, to say the least. Most people cannot do it all. But many women keep trying because they believe it is a failure and an admission of defeat to do less. In an effort to assert some control, they schedule chores, tasks, and commitments in day planners that leave few time slots for themselves. Although backlash against the title Superwoman surfaces periodically, women find it hard to surrender, to let go of things they feel they have to do or try to control.

Surrendering, however, doesn't mean defeat. It can be essential to freeing yourself from unnecessary shackles. Surrendering is about breaking free, about moving beyond where you are. Are you ready for your new opportunities and possibilities in your life? Surrendering provides one of them.

Surrender means to let go and let God. It is admitting your past mistakes and forgiving yourself for them, being willing to explore what you don't know, and asking for help and guidance. The operative word here is *willing*. You have to be willing to ask for help, not because you are weak but because you want to remain strong. Surrender includes self-acknowledgment of the fact that you not only have hopes and dreams, you also have fears and doubts. It is the most powerful state you can choose to be in. To surrender is a state of knowing that the power is within you, not outside of you. Whenever it appears to you that your power is elsewhere, you can reclaim your power by embracing your ability to surrender.

Sisters are too powerful not to change our circumstances. We are well positioned to transform our individual lives and also create a momentum that will lift our families and communities to an unprecedented level of economic, business, and entrepreneurial achievement in the twenty-first century.

Are you sick and tried of where you are right now, to

the point where you will stand up for yourself and declare your right to a better life? No matter whom you have to face, no matter what you have to do? Will you take it on? Are you ready to claim your rightful place in this world? You have to decide that it's not too late, that you deserve much more than you're putting up with, and that you are not willing to deny yourself any longer.

Declare an end to the struggle to make ends meet, going to a job you hate, having trouble managing money, and feeling overwhelmed with unwanted debt. Declare it is time to do something to change your situation. When you make this declaration and then take action, you regain the power to create the future you desire. Resolve that you will not be a spectator in life. Ask yourself, "What can I do today to make my life better?" Ask it and do it every day. Remember, you are your most important resource in making your life work.

Get out of the dependence cycle or the victim cycle. You may blame racism or sexism for your position in life. You may be waiting for someone to give you something. There are no handouts. Let success happen and make success happen; don't wait for success to happen.

Make the commitment to get the skills, discipline, and money management experience you need. Take full responsibility for your financial well-being. Get over feeling frustrated, irresponsible, and bad about yourself and your financial situation. My guess is that you have probably never had any real training in managing money. You can get some basic information about personal finance—setting up accounts, making deposits in person or by direct deposit, interest rates, reading financial statements—at your local bank. Check out your library or local bookstore for books on money, finance, and investing. If your debts are too great for your current resources, make an appointment at a credit counseling service that does not charge a fee. Getting information and applying the relevant parts to your situation will give you power over your finances.

Stop using "I don't know what to do or how to do it" as an excuse. Be committed to getting the information and support you need to manage your money. You might want to find a money management coach. Realize that your lack of knowledge can cost you money. Are you eligible for a credit card that charges a lower rate of interest than your current card? Can you get an insurance policy with the same coverage or value for a lower premium? Does your status as a woman, minority, or small business owner qualify you for financing opportunities?

Stop using "I've never been good with money" as an excuse. Replace your old money management habits with new ones. Be willing to admit what you do not know. And be willing to get the information you need. Read the business section of your newspaper. Take a class. You may need to ask for help in balancing your accounts, determining where your money goes, cutting your expenses, paying your bills on time, eliminating debt, clearing your credit report, investing in yourself, saving more money, and putting a financial structure in place.

You may be buying lottery tickets or ordering get-rich-quick tapes or spending lots of time scheming to win the lottery or the sweepstakes. Chasing the latest and greatest money-making opportunities allows denial to set in, and it costs too much, in both time and money. While you are creating the future, you have to live in the present, so don't get involved in activities and behaviors that won't allow you to live until the big deal happens or the money comes through.

What thoughts and beliefs do you have about money? The thoughts you hold about money have tremendous power, and the more responsible and abundant these thoughts are, the better. Talking about money can also be empowering. In our culture, unfortunately, it is taboo to talk about money issues. Financial problems are kept secret, even among family members. You can feel tremendous relief and freedom in sharing your concerns and questions with safe people. Whether it's friends and family or a professional accountant or a money management or life planning coach, we all need support and guidance in learning new financial skills. Get an objective, well-trained professional to bounce ideas off and to provide tax planning or estate planning advice. It does not have to cost you money to get the information. Perhaps you know a financial planner at your church who will give you a consultation if you provide a piano lesson.

Asking for help is the number one solution to the obstacle of denial and avoidance. Finding the help you need will make taking action much easier. It is important that the people with whom you choose to work are well suited to your personality. Pick someone you feel comfortable with, and who makes you feel empowered rather than intimidated because of his or her knowledge about money. Develop a partnership with someone who understands and respects you and your financial concerns. When you find yourself feeling fearful or not knowing what to do or moving in circles instead of moving forward, ask for help. You will learn that you are not alone; others share similar situations, fears, and concerns. Begin dialogues about money. Identify the specific areas you need help with when it comes to money. Then arrange to get help.

If you truly want to change, you must acknowledge that you create your own experience. Then you must analyze what you've done or haven't done to create the undesirable results you are experiencing. You have to acknowledge your actions. Ask yourself, What's going on in my life right now? I accept that I'm responsible, so what did I do to contribute to this situation? What choices did I make that led to this situation? What did I neglect to do? What actions do I now need to take in order to change? What do I need to do to start behaving in a more productive way?

By maintaining that you are a victim, you can insist that life is not fair, that someone is treating you wrong, or that you are being discriminated against. Or you can simply believe that you are right in your position and those who disagree with you are wrong, and therefore it is not your fault that things are the way they are. The bottom line is that you are not a victim unless you choose to be one. You have to own the current situation, accept it, and acknowledge it, in order to act on it.

Hiding something or denying your situation is not productive. The energy you are using to try to hide something challenges your authenticity. I am not saying you have to be perfect; I am saying that once you acknowledge and accept that you create your own experience, you stop being a victim. You can begin to consciously, purposefully, and actively create the experience you want instead of suffering through experiences you don't want.

It's time to stop making excuses and start making results. If you refuse to acknowledge your self-destructive behaviors, not only will they continue, they will gain momentum, become more deeply entrenched in the habitual patterns of your life, and grow more and more resistant to change.

If you are scared, then you must say "I am scared." If you are confused, admit it. Consider how refreshing it would be to wake up tomorrow and honestly be able to say, "For the first time in my life, I am not lying to myself. For the first time in my life, I am facing the honest truth."

Maybe you have loved, only to have your heart broken. You may have gone away from that situation with bitterness, resentment, hurt, and fear. Maybe you have been falsely accused and condemned by others, and that has left you angry, resentful, and bitter. Maybe you have lost a loved one, and that has left you questioning the fairness and justice of life, feeling distanced from God or generally skeptical. Maybe you are in a marriage or relationship that is marked by disharmony or hostility, and that has left you guarded and unwilling to be open and vulnerable. Maybe you doubt your self-worth or question whether you have the qualities that other people have, leaving you feeling scared and alone.

These are meaningful aspects of who you are, and if you ignore or deny the fact that these experiences have created characteristics in you that dictate how you interact with others, you are denying an important part of your life. If you do not acknowledge the presence of the characteristic or event, whatever it is, then you cannot and will not escape that experience; you cannot let go.

FORGIVENESS

Not letting go will keep you a prisoner of your past. No matter what happened, you did the best you could at the time. Accept and forgive yourself. Forgiving is an inner process, an act of love and compassion for yourself. It allows you to release the pain, emotion, and attachment to negative energy. Forgiveness will provide you with the opportunity to heal and allow you to love and be at peace with your personal history, instead of leading a life directed by guilt, shame, and anger. The ability to forgive both yourself and others is one of the most important components in healing past wounds. Do yourself a favor and forgive yourself. When you do, you can live an emotionally peaceful life, free from the victim mentality.

Forgiveness allows you to take your power back from those who have hurt you. Ill feelings can imprison you; forgiveness sets you free. You bring your thoughts, feelings, and beliefs into every relationship you have. When you let go of ill feelings, you bring a new and fresh perspective to your relationships—including your relationship with money.

You must forgive yourself for all of the dumb money mistakes you have made. Remember, if you had known how to do better, you would have done better.

Power lies in your attitude and your interpretation of life's situations. Make a list of all the reasons and justifications that you give yourself for being angry with yourself. Write a letter to yourself focusing on an area that you need to forgive yourself for. Remember that you are human and, therefore, you make mistakes. You've held on to guilt and shame long enough to learn from them. You don't need to punish yourself any longer. You deserve to move on with your life.

LETTING GO OF THE PAST

True wealth is based on the willingness and the ability to let go and move on. In order to grow and have something you want that you don't have, in order to learn something new, you have to release the old and let go of things from the past. Many people are attached to what they have—the familiar, the known, the comfortable. Although they say they want something new, they cling like crazy to what they have. You have to let go before you can get new things. If you want something, you have to create a space for it. You may need to let go of how you work, whom you work with, or unproductive relationships. Look at where you are too attached and look at what you are clinging to. You can be emotionally attached to something that has long ceased to be of value, but you may not be willing to give it up.

The ability to let go is a cornerstone of true wealth.

It takes a winner to know when to change directions and when enough is enough. If you give something your best and it still isn't working out, you can consider it a victory to move on.

How do you leave and let go? It is going to take effort. It may take one action, or several small steps, to get you moving in the right direction. But you cannot move forward until you let go. It may be scary and uncomfortable, and it's not going to be easy, but it is necessary.

Think about a way of working, a way of relating, a way of handling your money or relationships that you could give up because it is outdated. Then discover a way of working, a way of relating, a way of handling your money or relationships that you would like to adopt. You can discover new approaches to handling money through books, courses, or the Internet. You can also write about your ideas for change in a journal or share them with a support group. Release what narrows your life and constricts it. Embrace that which expands your abilities, knowledge, and life, and gets you closer to true wealth.

Letting go doesn't have to be dramatic. Every time you say "no," you are letting go of something. Every time you delegate, you are letting go of something. Every time you hire a baby-sitter or independent contractor, you are letting go of having to do everything yourself. You may have to let go so everyone can be served. Letting go suggests moving on and a willingness to have closure and completeness. By letting go, you create space for new options and possibilities.

Paradoxically, loss can open up new opportunities.

Losing a job or going into retirement gives an opportunity to find a new beginning. Loss does not necessarily have to represent a sense of scarcity. Your perception of your loss needs to be reshaped to lead to inner growth.

Do whatever you have been postponing or putting off. The goal is to become fulfilled. Give up feeling worthless, unworthy, not good enough, not deserving, hopeless, not qualified, or helpless. Let go of fear, anxiety, guilt, and confusion about money. After you let go, your actions will create your authentic journey.

You Did the Best You Knew How

Embarrassment, shame, or guilt related to past experiences and behaviors can be paralyzing. Don't let the shame of the past affect your present behavior. Acknowledge that you may have made a mistake, but you are not a mistake.

Accept and recognize that you made choices and engaged in behaviors, and therefore you are responsible for the results. Maya Angelou once said, "You did what you knew how to do, and when you knew better, you did better."

Whatever your past habits and your patterns of behavior may be, you must recognize that you no longer need to live your life that way. Beginning again may require you to take risks by trying out new behavior that goes against the way you have been in the past. You may make mistakes when you try a new approach, but failure is not fatal. Mistakes are no reason for misery. Our mistakes can be the most powerful teachers we have. Learning from mistakes gives real wisdom. Instead of blaming and judging yourself for your errors, you can choose new behaviors and move on.

To complete your past so that you can move into the future, most advice tells us to accept that we get to be who we are as a result of the past, that we are shaped by the events that happened around us and to us. I believe those past events might shape us, but they do not have to become us or define us.

Recently, a female executive retained me as her business coach. She was frustrated because she had been unable to get a promotion. She did everything the books said to do to be successful, win friends, and influence people. After the first two sessions, I noticed that she had a habit of saying things like "I did the stupidest thing" or "You wouldn't believe this stupid thing I did." As I talked with her about why she referred to her actions in that way, she grew puzzled as to why these phrases infiltrated her language. Slowly, with coaching, she revealed that people whose opinions she respected had called her stupid when she was a girl. She believed them and internalized that belief. Although she graduated from high school and college, got a job, and received promotions into management, she was still haunted by her past. She convinced herself that her achievements were not the result of her being smart, but of her being lucky. The skills she had gained were not a sign of her hard work, because anyone could learn the skills if *she* could. After all, she was stupid. Being haunted by her past resulted in a lack of self-esteem, and she fell into a pattern of depression, not because she was stupid but because she did not believe in herself and the ability that she possessed and demonstrated.

I asked her to consider re-evaluating some of the events and circumstances that had happened in her past and might be shaping the way she feels about herself in the present. I asked her to forgive herself for the things that had happened that she was not proud of. She needed to understand that she had done the best she could under the circumstances; if she had known better, she would have done better. I asked her to consider changing the language she used and the conversations she had about herself. I reminded her that self-talk, the conversations we have with and about ourselves to ourselves, has an impact on the way we communicate with others and the way others communicate with us. I encouraged her to look at her positive attributes, and she said she couldn't think of very many. So I asked her to tell me what kind of compliments others gave her. Then, I asked her to own those compliments and accept them as the truth. By letting go of negative perceptions formed when she was younger, and accepting a new perspective, she was able to heal past wounds.

It is important to be aware that the events in your daily life have only the meaning that you assign to them. We all view the world through our paradigms or filters. The presence of these filters is neither good nor bad; it just is. You need to recognize the presence of your filters, and be sure they don't distort your perceptions and mislead you in your decision-making. Many people operate as if facts and their interpretations of facts are one and the same thing. They observe a fact, make up an interpretation or a story about it, and then act as if the interpretation is a fact.

For example, if you open a small business and wind up in bankruptcy, you might interpret this as the world saying to you, "You aren't worthy of our business, our money, our support. We reject you and your efforts or products." By examining the facts you may find that you may have needed more training or your location wasn't good or that any one of a number of factors could have caused the bankruptcy.

If you apply negative filters to future endeavors, you will most probably fail. Remember, it doesn't matter whether your past was good or bad, just that it was. If you view the world through a filter created by past events, you will allow your past to control and dictate both your present and your future.

Ask yourself, *Through what filters do I view the world?* Then exercise your flexibility and get rid of the fixed beliefs that may be holding you back. Separate facts (events, actions, deeds) from interpretations (what you think they meant or what others told you they meant) to remove filters from your perception of your life or abilities.

CHALLENGES

By accepting and acknowledging the truth in your life, you commit yourself to resolving rather than enduring your personal challenges. If you're the kind of person who addresses everyone else's challenges and needs, but don't take care of your own, you are headed for emotional bankruptcy. You must resolve to devote a substantial amount of your problem-solving to your own issues. Remember, you can't give away what you don't have.

UNFINISHED BUSINESS

Before you can move on to wealth, you must resolve any unfinished business. This may include paying or arranging to pay off bills or communicating with people you have not kept your promises to.

Do what the credit counselor says: pick one bill and pay it off completely, week by week or month by month. Also, keep your priorities in order. Do not overspend for birthdays, Christmas, or other holidays. Maintain your car so it won't break down and leave you with a major repair bill that causes you to lose sight of your dream by falling into another debt trap.

Refuse to live with unfinished emotional business. Identify when you are hurting, angry, frustrated, or confused, then call time out and deal with it. Address the problem with the person it involves or at least with yourself. If emotional pains or problems have cluttered your life, you must insist on getting closure. Closure means not carrying the problem or the pain with you. Whatever that takes, do it. It may mean confronting yourself or the other person. It may mean forgiveness or making an apology. Avoid piling up this kind of burden in your life; give yourself emotional closure.

Honor your promises, commitments, and agreements, whether they're with yourself or others. Think about how you feel when someone makes a commitment to you and then breaks it. Have the courage to ask yourself what agreements you have broken with the people you care about. Don't make promises and commitments and then not honor them. Whether you intend the message or not, you tell yourself you are not important and it tells others that they are not important to you. It says to them that they have been rejected. You may not realize the obstacles you have put in your way by being unreliable. Broken agreements create pain and distance, and that affects you. Start by honoring commitments to yourself, your family, and then to your creditors.

Successful people's lives have shown us over and over again that the quality of their lives is determined not by what happened to them, but by how they responded to what happened to them. The Sister I coached needed to shift her perception of herself. She needed to forgive herself for her self-doubt. But this requires hard work. And in order to make the shift, you have to be committed to doing the work.

As you strive to make changes in your life, remember and rely on the Serenity Prayer: "God, grant me the serenity to accept the things I cannot change, the courage to change the things I can, and the wisdom to know the difference."

Following are some actions you can take when you surrender yourself to the process of forgiving yourself for past mistakes and moving on.

- Balance your accounts. Use your checkbook ledger, ATM receipts, and bank statements.

- Know where your money goes—keep a daily accounting so you know where the dollars go.

- Cut your expenses—for a week, get a receipt for everything you spend money on. Then divide the receipts into two piles: (1) items you needed or that provided a benefit to you and (2) those that weren't needed or beneficial.

- Pay your bills on time—bills come first, entertainment second.

- Eliminate debt—Debtors Anonymous has chapters across the country. You can even access its services on the Internet.

- Repair your credit—get a copy of your credit report and write an explanation about anything that is unfavorable. (Did you miss payments because you were unemployed or sick for a long time? Is someone else's bad credit reflected on your report?) The best repair is to pay bills in full and on time.

- Start saving—you can develop a personal savings plan that takes into account your current budget and income as well as future needs. Remember to invest in your future, which is also an investment in yourself.

Surrendering is a powerful tool to help you clear the way toward your wealth-creation journey.

Chapter Eleven

❦

Shifting: The Be-Do-Have Paradigm

SHIFTING is making a move away from where you are and closer to where you want to be. This step is important as part of the strategies you need for achieving your dreams. Shifting may require shifting from a poverty consciousness to a wealth-creating consciousness. For example:

- Believing in abundance rather than believing in scarcity

- Focusing on what you love and want rather than focusing on what you dislike and you don't want

- Thinking of how you will create money rather than focusing on how you need money

- Remembering past successes rather than remembering past failures

- Acknowledging how far you have come rather than focusing on how far you have to go

- Measuring wealth as fulfilling your purpose rather than how much money you have

- Giving and receiving freely rather than not giving or being open to receive

- Expecting the best to happen rather than worrying that the worst will happen

- Doing your best rather than cutting corners

- Discovering how you can serve others rather than only on what others will give you

- Applauding others' success rather than feeling threatened by others' success

As you work on shifting, questions you might want to consider are:

Where am I now?

Where do I want to be in the future?

What's missing?

What can I do to close this gap?

What becomes possible for me when I close the gap?

Shifting also requires examining the way you approach what you do for a living. Ask yourself the following questions:

What do I love to do most?

How can I make a living doing what I love?

How can I create more value in the work that I do to benefit others?

Whatever the answers are to those questions, stand up, claim them, and develop a strategy to make the shift. Look at what you want to be, do, and have, and act on it. In order to get all aspects of your life on track, you have to align your behaviors (being) with your work and activities (doing).

WHY MAKE A SHIFT?

Right now, your actions and behavior are not bringing you the results that you desire and need. You need to shift or move away from those actions and behaviors in order to get different and better results.

Remember, the pain of the past was probably caused by the condition you want to change. If the change you need to make is to make more money, the pain of the past might be recalled by remembering those times when you wanted to buy your children or some other family member something they needed but you couldn't afford it.

Also, the pain in your present may be caused by the condition that you want to change. That pain may be causing you sleepless nights or embarrassing situations with your creditors. But that pain is a message telling you it is time to pay attention and make a change. You can use pain to build or strengthen your commitment to shift to a better path.

Imagine all the pleasure you will get in the future by *cashing in* and creating true wealth in your life.

For example, let's look at two equally qualified working women. One is a Sister; the other is a Sista. One is successful and the other is not, not because of anything either is doing, but because of what both are *being*.

The Sister is being caring, sharing, open, helpful, considerate, cheerful, friendly, confident, even joyful in her work, while the Sista is being closed, distant, uncaring, inconsiderate, jealous, grumpy, even resentful of what she is doing.

The Sista just *knows* that if she only had a little more money, she'd be truly happy. She does not understand the connection between "not being very happy" right now and not having the money she wants. She doesn't know she already has everything she needs to be happy. Most people believe that if they "have" a thing (more money, time, love—whatever), they can finally "do" a thing (write a book, buy a home, go on vacation), which will allow them to "be" a thing (happy, content, peaceful).

In actuality, they are reversing the Be-Do-Have paradigm. Having does not produce being; it's the other way around.

First you must "be" the thing called "happy" (or wise, compassionate, and so on); then you will start doing things from this place of beingness. Soon you will discover that what you are doing brings you the things you've always wanted to "have." "Beingness" attracts "doingness" and "doingness" produces "havingness."

The way to put this process into motion is to look at what you want to have and ask yourself what you think you would "be" if you had it, then go ahead and "be" that. Act as if you have already attained your goal, and it will be that much closer to your grasp. Here is a short way to state this principle: To *cash in*, you do not have to "do" anything. You have to "be" something—happy, caring, sharing, and so on.

The formula for taking purposeful action is: Be, Do, Have. Be committed, Do what it takes, and you will Have what you want. Until knowledge, awareness, insights, and understanding are translated into action, they are of no value.

A shift in attitudes and awareness will have an impact on your "beingness." As your consciousness changes, your life will change. If you want money, wealth, love, or prosperity, act as if you already have those attributes and you will draw them to you. When you act as if you are, you become. Your actions have to be sincere, however, or the benefit of the action is lost.

To break through the cycle you are in and to move forward, you have to shift your focus from what you don't want to what you do want. This may be hard at first because you are used to accepting less than what you deserve or getting by with what is handed to you. By focusing on what you want, you will be happy inside so you can be, do, and have what you want on the outside. You will move beyond buying things you don't need or having to have material things to look good and feel good. No longer competitive for competition's sake, you will be able to build the life you want. You will accomplish your personal goals, dreams, and aspirations, not those someone else wants for you. You will make all of your dreams come true by being honest with yourself, forgiving yourself, loving yourself, and honoring your goals and aspirations. I once heard Rev. Jeremiah Wright

say, "God will not give you a vision without a provision."
I believe that if there is something that you really want,
it really wants you, too.

As you shift and change, you are going to behave differently and do things you have not done before. You
are going to shift your approach to the way you see yourself, your work and career, the way you invest your
money, the way you plan for retirement. The territory
you're entering is new. It's unknown; it's not part of your
present life. Be willing to experiment and try new things.
Don't worry if change doesn't happen overnight.

The difference between the Sisters who are fulfilled
and those who are not fulfilled is that fulfilled Sisters
will take chances and take purposeful, meaningful action;
they don't just think about it. If you change what you
do, and you manage the trade-offs you get, you are moving in the right direction. Nothing in your life will
change until you begin to do different things, whether
that means becoming interested in the stock market,
starting a new exercise program, or going back to school.
Your actions will gain momentum. You'll meet new people; new possibilities will come to you.

Make the shift to make yourself the most important
person in your life. If you take care of yourself, then you
have something to give to your children, other loved
ones, or the people who depend on you.

Cashing in with purpose and commitment will cause
you to look, feel, and be different. You will start living
proactively instead of reactively. Remember, the only
difference between you and the people who already have
what they want is that they took a different course of

action. You may have settled too early and too cheaply. Staying in your comfort zone can be hazardous to your future. To get your life to flow differently, you will need to change what you think, feel, and do in order to be focused but flexible. Remember a simple truth: If you keep doing what you're doing, you're going to keep getting what you're getting.

To restore your financial health, raise your standards! Shift your attitude from "Dealing with money is too much work or too confusing" to "I'll do whatever it takes to restore my financial health." When you take the necessary *actions* to get on track, you end up feeling good about yourself, and that's the key ingredient to *cashing in*. When you feel secure about the way you handle money, you naturally attract more. You will ask for the money you deserve, ask for a raise, increase your fee.

The growth of a woman from princess to queen, from Sista to Sister, is part of the miracle of our feminine transformation. It begins with a shift in desire, a decision to change, a willingness to do God's work, and a commitment to follow your vision.

In 1977, I was with a couple of women in an office in a downtown Detroit hotel. We were all complaining about the lack of resources available to Black women in business. We were trying to help ourselves, but we also had an authentic need and desire to serve all Black women. When we created our own resource and founded the National Association of Black Women Entrepreneurs (NABWE), one of the first things NABWE did was to ask for a meeting with the president of the United States. And we got it. We used our collective power and got to go to the White House! Now, if we had been *Sistas*, we would have kept complaining—and nothing would have happened until a true *Sister* came along to take action and make the commitment necessary to get something done!

You have the power to say what is or is not possible in your future. What you say is possible determines what is possible. Your actions, and the results they produce, are a reflection of the future you envision for yourself.

When you alter the way you are being, with effectiveness and competence, you gain the capacity to make the impossible real. You have to create a new framework—the vision you created for yourself—from which you relate to the world.

One way to alter your way of being is by altering the conversations you engage in. Saying "I'm broke" is no longer acceptable. When people around you talk about how broke they are, insist that they change their language. Power will be generated by this collective stand. You could be temporarily out of cash or having cash flow challenges, but you are not broke. This subtle shift in language will contribute to a change in your perception of your situation. It's not denying a money problem but reframing it so that it can be more easily addressed and overcome. You are embarking on a new journey. What you have learned or done in the past won't help you with the task before you.

To make the shift to the new "being," ask yourself the following questions:

- What would I like to do, but I'm not committed to now, only because I don't believe I can do it?

- What am I not actively taking on, but would if I could?

- What am I interested in accomplishing that requires reinventing myself to accomplish it?

- What would I be committed to accomplishing— if only it were possible?

- What's worth accomplishing—so much so that it would be worth reinventing my whole self?

When you have shifted your focus from what's happening now to what you want for the future, you have made a powerful change in your life. It may seem like a small step, but it is an important one.

Meet Dorothy and Patricia, who are continually pressured by money troubles. They never seem to have enough. Not only do I hear them talk about how broke they are, I can see it in their behaviors, in their attitudes, in the way they speak about their condition. They have become convinced that it is impossible for them to exist in any other way. "We were born with money troubles," they say, "and we will go to our graves with them— unless, of course, something impossible happens."

Now suppose that Dorothy and Patricia make the declaration, "We declare that if we say something is possible, then it is. We declare there is no scarcity of money." This declaration shifts the boundaries of their future. In the past, Dorothy and Patricia had taken financial planning courses without success, which may have helped convince them that they would always have money troubles. Previously, they focused on their outer selves before their inner selves. Now, they recognize that they will have to do the inner work to shift their way of being before any financial planning courses will do them some good. Their new perspective on money is, "There is no scarcity of money." This is now the context—the environment—for their actions with money. When they took financial planning courses in the past, they were acting from the belief that there is never enough money. This time, the same actions—taking financial planning courses—are being taken inside of a new framework, a new realm of possibility that didn't exist before—the possibility that there is no scarcity of money. Now there is an environment in which taking financial planning courses can make a difference.

Someone outside Dorothy and Patricia's experience would recognize the possibility of no scarcity of money immediately—after all, many people with less income than Dorothy and Patricia manage to live without constant money troubles. Dorothy and Patricia had to recognize the possibility themselves; they reached this recognition only after they made a declaration about their own influence over the possibility of their own future.

Take a stand—commit yourself to act consistently with the vision or possibility you declare for yourself, from the moment the declaration is spoken, regardless of the circumstances. After taking this stand and making the commitment, all the deterrents of the past—interpretation, historical analysis, and fear—exist no longer.

Once you declare your vision, ask yourself: "What actions do I take next to move this forward to a reality? What's missing and essential right now?"

Be willing to give up suffering and struggle in order to expand your vision. Taking the time to allow your vision to broaden will bring clarity to your vision. You have to be patient. Don't be tempted to rush and skip steps, using the belief or excuse that time is money or that speed is more important than the direction in which you travel.

For many years, we have accepted an extremely limited vision of ourselves as essentially weak, powerless, dependent, and subject to innumerable forces and circumstances beyond our control. Look beyond this limited vision and begin in earnest to discover who you are—a woman with no limitations and immeasurable potential. Your willingness to feel this power will enable you to realize that you are not at the mercy of circumstances beyond your control; rather, you are the creator of those circumstances. You achieve a new vantage point from which you see more opportunity.

Madame C. J. Walker was what futurist Joel Barker calls a paradigm pioneer. When she started her company, there were already hair care products on the market, but they weren't working, so she decided to create her own. She took someone else's idea, embellished it, and made it more successful. She created a new standard of beauty for the Black woman and left a legacy that is still helping us today. She didn't do it for herself. She did it for the generations following her, so young girls and boys could see their own beauty and possibilities.

A paradigm shift occurs when the rules change as a result of an individual discovering a new pattern for problem-solving, whether with an innovation or a new idea. As a result of a paradigm shift, the standard way of doing business can become obsolete or irrelevant. Shifting a paradigm means fundamentally altering the way things are done. This will require you to get outside of the box you have been operating in, and to be willing to break your own rules of past success.

Chapter Twelve

Simplifying: Achieving Harmony in Your Life

SIMPLIFYING is a balancing act that involves every area of your life and ensures that your many roles are in harmony. When your roles conflict with each other, it can drain your time, energy, money, and other resources. Within each role, goals define what you want to achieve.

You have several roles in your life. The financial dimension is only one piece of the puzzle. However, the more trouble you have with money, the more energy this struggle will take from you and the more challenging it will be to live the life you want. Examining only the material approach or aspects of life leaves us spiritually empty and emotionally unfulfilled. You cannot enjoy a peaceful and constructive life if you have competing agendas, with one part of you serving one master, and some other part serving another. For a Sister to really *cash in*, you need to find ways to develop and express all aspects of who you are.

I've identified twelve key areas of life where attention and action are needed: Personal, Interpersonal, Organizational, Spiritual, Mental/Educational, Emotional, Physical, Political, Legal, Technical, Social, and Environmental. If you are going to measure your progress, you must be willing to examine every area in your life. But where to begin? Usually, wherever you are unfulfilled, in pain, struggling, or feeling inadequate or incomplete may serve as a guide as to where to begin.

The life you are managing is your own and has unique facets that must be considered carefully. Making decisions in an informed, purposeful way will create and generate what you want. While you are changing, be fearless and be careful not to confuse the means with the end. While focusing on what you want to be, do, and have, take the time and attention to identify how that object or event would make you feel. Always question your wants and desires. You may realize that it's not the thing or the event that you really want but the feelings that you associate with it.

There may be many paths that will arrive at the same destination. But to find the right way, you must be as specific as possible and make sure that the path you follow suits all aspects of your life. While each aspect of your life may certainly influence the others, each one also has distinct life dimensions that are worthy of separate considerations.

You may have goals and objectives in all twelve categories. Examine each one and ask yourself, "Where am

I currently, and what do I truly want in the future?"
You'll need to consider each category even if you believe
you are on solid ground in that area of your life. If you
are satisfied with your current status in that category,
verify that your perception is true and then move on to
other areas.

On a scale of 1–10, rate yourself in the different areas.
Are you performing that role to the best of your ability?
Are you fully satisfied and happy in that position? You
want to operate from a position of strength rather than
weakness, because then you will be functioning with
knowledge instead of ignorance. Dreaming, wishing, and
wanting should be considered when you evaluate each
dimension. What delights you and makes your heart
sing? What admired person in your life is creating and
generating successful results in the roles you are performing? It is worth the time to study their attitudes and
actions.

The ultimate goal is integration of aspects of your life
by developing and balancing yourself at all levels. When
all levels of your life are in balance, you will have
achieved a more simplified lifestyle.

PERSONAL

This level involves the relationship you have with yourself. This is where you develop personal trustworthiness,
character, values, and integrity. Everything on the
wealth-creation journey starts with the self. LEAP deals
with self-development. In this relationship, you want a
personal compass that always keeps you headed true

north, in the direction that matters most to you. For example, you may decide you are not willing to sacrifice time with family and friends for travel required to advance in your career.

INTERPERSONAL

This covers relationships and interactions with others. In interpersonal relationships, you want to develop trustworthiness and connection with others. Ask forgiveness for past mistakes and misunderstandings. Make commitments to honor your agreements and relationships.

ORGANIZATIONAL

The ability to organize people, build teams, solve problems, and create aligned visions, goals, structures, strategies, and systems is part of your organizational area. When you are in alignment with the organization and your coworkers, you will be empowered. You will also enhance your management skills. Interfacing with the community you live in, perhaps through community services or volunteer work, is also an expression of organizational networks in your life.

SPIRITUAL

Spirituality represents the inner essence, the deeper meaning and purpose in life, and provides the foundation for the development of the other levels. Spirituality represents your sense of interrelatedness with all beings. Spiritual emptiness is at the core of most social, political, and environmental crises. Spirituality can give you inspiration and courage to face yourself and the changes you need to make in your life.

MENTAL/EDUCATIONAL

Intellect (the ability to think and reason, thoughts, attitudes, ideas, viewpoints, beliefs, and values) and basic life philosophy are found in the mental or educational part of yourself. Your mind enables you to gather knowledge and wisdom from your life experience and from the world around you. Learn how to learn. Learn what you need to learn for your particular endeavors.

Old ideas, beliefs, and values that you still want to hold on to will no longer serve you or your well-being. Be prepared to let them go and make room for new ways of thinking and doing.

EMOTIONAL

Through emotion, you have the ability to experience life deeply and to relate to others and the world on a feeling level. This level seeks meaningful contact and connection with others—a sense of family, community, and belonging. This facet of your life also allows you to be in touch with your feelings and be able to say how you feel authentically about your feelings and your purpose.

PHYSICAL

The physical body is important in your ability to survive and thrive in the material world. You should learn to take good care of your body by listening to it carefully, feeding it when it's hungry, exercising, getting enough sleep, and not abusing your body with drugs or chemicals. The healthier you are, the more energy you'll feel.

POLITICAL

It is often said that if you are not in politics, you are not in business. Become more aware of and involved in the social and political issues in your community. Ask yourself how you might best use your time, energies, and talents to serve the larger world. Our inner cities are filled with millions of people, primarily African Americans, living under social and economic conditions as desperate as those during the worst days of the Great Depression. Utilize your right to vote. Leverage your purchasing power. Let your voice be heard by actively supporting businesses that are aligned with your values and boycotting companies that oppose them.

LEGAL

Obeying the law and acting as an example for your children and other family members falls within the legal area. Upholding just laws is an essential part of an orderly society.

TECHNICAL

Keeping up in a changing technological world seems to get harder every day. Trillions of dollars are going into worldwide technology during the next few years. To prepare yourself to take advantage of the opportunities this will present, read, get on-line, and become literate about E-mail, the Internet, and the World Wide Web.

SOCIAL

Fun is important. You can do it all and have it all while having a ball. The social side of you is the side that is nurtured by play, which can be anything from competing in sports to going to movies to relaxing at the beach. Social activities are crucial to recharging your batteries.

ENVIRONMENTAL

Is your environment conducive to *cashing in*? This means your house, your car, your office. Do you have the tools, the space, the comfort from which to launch your wealth-creation journey?

These twelve areas are relevant in your life regardless of whether you are in the start-up, growth, or expansion stage of your career or business. These areas have to be examined and re-examined as you grow and expand. Because we work, most of us are familiar with or have heard talk related to business development. It's common to hear people say that a business is in a start-up phase, which means the business is just opening its doors and getting started. We might hear later that the business has undergone growth or that its growth stage has led it to expand. Just like a business, you can be in different stages of development. As you grow and expand as a person, your career and business will grow and expand. Your greatest teacher for personal growth and development is the lessons you learn from living life, including your perceived failures. Make a habit of asking yourself, "What lesson was I supposed to learn from that experience? Did I get it?"

When you expand your vision for wealth (beyond cash and possessions) in each dimension of your life, you will find yourself connecting to your inner spirit and feeling whole and complete. As you continue the journey, you will find you are capable of creating new ideas and turning concepts into reality. It is important to learn to trust and rely on your intuitive judgments. Intuition, courage, and commitment are the long-term qualities you need to be successful. An act of faith may be required to make a change, but it may also lead you to a great reward.

To simplify your life, determine why you want to acquire money, launch a project, change jobs, become self-employed, go to school, travel, spend more time on your spiritual life, or take time off to write and explore.

Knowing what you want will give you clarity about the needs it will fulfill. But be open to alternative outcomes to your original vision. Many things other than what you picture might give you the essence of what you want, so let what you want come in whatever way, size, shape, or form that is most appropriate.

We have to have money, but it is helpful to simplify our lives to such an extent that our emotions surrounding money are in a state of freedom and balance, and are in alignment with the other dimensions of our lives. If you shift the focus to your role in generating money, and away from the money itself, you will be empowered and less of a slave to accumulating money for money's sake. The clearer you paint that picture, the more likely you are to achieve it.

Another key is to act from a sense of urgency and realize that the time you have been wasting is your own. Your future is at stake. You want to create *opportunities* and *possibilities* for yourself that allow all aspects of your life to operate in harmony.

You can't allow yourself to be detoured by psychic benefits, things that look good or impress others, like a corner office, an impressive title, a larger facility or a bigger staff. Your main goal is to be able to take advantage of opportunities as soon as they appear. That's because opportunities won't last long in the information age: Windows of opportunity will open and shut more quickly than ever before.

All levels of your life are equally important. You cannot afford to neglect any of them. For instance, if you have done a great deal of spiritual work but ignored the other levels, you may become so spiritual that you are no earthly good. The levels are interrelated, and any work you do on one affects all the others. If you don't deal with each level as a separate but integral piece of the wholesome fulfillment of your life, lifestyle, and livelihood, or pay attention to some aspect but ignore others, you may feel empty, stuck, frustrated, or full of longing.

Once you understand where you are and where you want to be in each area of your life, you can begin to discover the options for creating wealth that best fit you and the future you want to create.

FINDING THE OPTION FOR CREATING WEALTH THAT FITS YOU

Wealth-creating options include business ventures, investments, entrepreneurship, intrapreneurship, multi-level marketing, home-based business, doing something "on the side" while working a traditional job, or being a professional practitioner.

While considering options, recall and reflect on anything you might consider a lost opportunity, something that was available to you that you didn't take advantage of, and see if you can re-create the essence of it into your life. This may be something you saw someone else accomplish. It may mean choosing work that has meaning to you and allowing yourself to bring your full self into your work and make a living while making a difference. Identifying what you have to offer and what's missing from your skills and knowledge should also be considered.

In creating options for yourself, you have to consider the right time to leave or let go. Feeling discontented, undervalued, or not the best you can be is an indication it is time to move on. Restlessness comes from denying yourself by not using your God-given skills and talents.

The more skillful you are, the more you have to contribute. Maybe working harder, longer, and with more effort is not the only way. Maybe you can work effortlessly by letting go of hard work and struggle. Be obedient, smart, wise, and intuitive enough to develop dreams and desires and parts of yourself that have been ignored, and find inner peace.

❦

Chapter Thirteen

Structuring: A Frame for Your Life

IT'S now time to begin translating your insights, understandings, and awareness into purposeful, meaningful, constructive actions. Start by committing to measure your life and its quality based on results, not intentions. To know why you are not completing any endeavor is half the challenge. The other half involves measuring yourself by results, by the bottom line, which will give you the information you need to make changes.

If you are going to start measuring your life based on results, that means you can't accept excuses from yourself or other people. Intention goes only so far. You must hold yourself to achieving results. Develop your own standards of acceptability. If the standards you set for yourself are too high or too low, which will probably be determined by trial and error, you're adding to your difficulties. Decide what you will demand from yourself versus what you are willing to accept from yourself. The standard you adopt for yourself should be one that you do not have to re-create every day.

Do you really have a strategy in your life, or are you just reactively going from day to day, taking what comes? Developing a structure is a way to keep score and be accountable for your life. Look at your lifestyle and habits. Are your habits contributing to what you want to accomplish? Become aware of your habits and behaviors regarding money. If they are not satisfactory, develop a financial structure that includes rituals, routines, saving, spending, sharing, and budgeting. Write it down. Make a commitment to follow your new game plan.

You have to trust your ability to construct answers for what you want and learn how to use your own ingenuity. If you don't know what to do, you must know that you have the wherewithal to get the answers you need. Self-respect or a feeling of trust is within you even though you may not have material wealth. You don't have to achieve overnight. You need to create a structure, or plan, that will take you step by step on your journey. That structure can develop over time. Just like an architect, you have to build a model of what you want to achieve. Ask yourself: "What would it look like, feel like, or be like if I had the solution?" Immerse yourself in possible solutions. Don't slip into the drama of your problem. Daydream. Keep a journal of your thoughts, goals, desires. Talk with others about what you are trying to achieve. Saying it out loud can reaffirm your commitment. Saturate your awareness with what you want, and examine your goal from as many different angles as possible. You are building answers as well as building the structure that will get you what you want. Dreaming alone won't do it, so you'll need to take action within a structured framework.

Desire is a message from your subconscious, and the methods for achieving what you desire are already in your possession. However, you may *feel* your direction more than you *know* what it is. Take the time to let your feelings and intuition guide you. Take sabbaticals from your daily life to allow room for daydreaming.

It is also important to set aside the time to create the proper structure to make your dreams come true. If you don't have a game plan in place, that lack will cause you to stop and start, impeding your best intentions. Put order, structure, and discipline in your life. Discipline comes from valuing whom you say you want to be, holding true to your vision for yourself, and not compromising. You have to be willing to give to yourself freely, which will increase your ability to "have." If you can't discipline yourself to save money, you won't have any. It's that simple.

Little things make a difference. Daily habits and rituals like prayer, meditation, preparation, listening, relationship-building, and ongoing value clarification are maintenance activities that help you take care of yourself. While they seem easy to push aside, they are exactly the things that will make the difference in the results you produce. Not engaging in these activities increases stress and frustration that are counterproductive to making your financial dreams come true.

List specific daily actions that support what you want. Schedule these activities in your day by choosing a specific time and place to do them. Choose as many as you can daily. Your list should reflect both business and personal actions that support your well-being. These daily actions are steps that will create the framework that will support your goals.

You also have to determine *who* you have to be to accomplish each goal. Your "who list" might say: "To reach this goal, I have to be someone who values and respects money, someone who hangs out with financially secure people, someone who spends and saves her money wisely, someone who has mastered investment language, someone who is willing to set financial goals, and someone who believes in abundance instead of scarcity." Developing the "who list" challenges you to go beyond your comfort zone. It stretches you; it asks you to become more. It also gives you a concrete image of who and what you want to be.

Trust yourself to do what matters most. Give yourself credit. Making and keeping promises to yourself precede making and keeping promises to others. Of course, you should not neglect your other commitments. Continue to monitor your alignment with universal principles, and fill in the details of what needs to be done. Every day find some way to improve an aspect of your structure and the process by which it is created.

Communicate your dreams and goals to like-minded people who will support you in making your dreams come true. Choose these people carefully and tell them what you are up to. Hold yourself accountable for your intentions, voice your goals out loud, and make a verbal commitment.

Through fulfilling your promises and commitments you will start to generate freedom, wealth, and power around money. You will be able to pay your bills on time, meet deadlines, complete what you started simply because you gave your word to do so. Goals are promises you make to yourself. Powerful goals have five qualities, represented by the acronym SMART. Each quality must be present for an item to qualify as a goal.

S is for specific. The goal for each of your roles must be explicit and precise.

M is for measurable. You must know when you have accomplished your goal.

A is for attainable. A goal needs to be a stretch for you but not impossible.

R is for relevant. Your goals must relate to one of your visions or intentions. It must be relevant to who you are and who you want to be.

T is for time-based. You must anchor your goal in time by giving it a date by which it will be accomplished.

When you are creating your goals, they must be specific, so you know where they begin and where they end. They must be measurable, so you will know if you have accomplished them. They must be attainable, so you will know if they support what you want to accomplish. They must be relevant, so you can determine whether or not your actions will really achieve the goal. And they must exist in time on your calendar, so you will know if you have completed your task within the specified time period. Instead of saying you want to make more money, say how much money you want to have by what period of time. Expressing your goal in measurable outcomes will let you know where you are, what still needs to be done, and if you have attained your goal.

Assign a time line to your goal. Goals require a particular schedule or calendar for their achievement. Be as specific as you can, so you can differentiate between dreams and goals. A dream statement might be, "I want to be rich before I die." A goal statement might be, "I want to make $50,000 by my fortieth birthday, in two years." Goals with time requirements do not allow for procrastination. Regardless of the time required to accomplish a goal, create a date by which it will be accomplished. For example, if your goal is to save $5,000 in twelve months, you can set milestones throughout the calendar year toward achieving your ultimate goal. By doing this, you will know when you are on track and when you need to make adjustments. Milestones make fulfillment possible. They let you know what you are committed to complete by a certain date. You will be monitoring yourself by saying, "I said this would happen by now. Did it happen?"

Choose a goal you can manage and plan a program or strategy that will help you get to your goal. This can be as simple as a daily to-do list. The more concrete your plans, the more you can rely on structure, not willpower, to get what you want. Arrange your environment so that it contributes to the results you desire. Identify those places, times, situations, and circumstances that set you up for failure by undermining your commitment to your plan or by reinforcing actions that detract from it. Reprogram those scenarios so when they pop up, they will not compete with what you really have to do.

Identify the specific time each day, and how much time per day you will spend working toward your goal, and put it in your schedule. Identify the physical location where you will be at the appointed time. Be specific, and your actions will pay off. Remember the rule of the game: If you are not taking the action, you will not have the outcomes you say you want.

Having a way to monitor your actions keeps you in motion. They let you know what you have to do to create the fulfillment of your dreams. They let you know if you did these things that "could" produce the results you want. By putting structure in your life, you have a clear-cut, day-to-day method of reviewing your progress toward your dreams. Creating a structure will allow you to develop concrete, achievable, tangible goals, the methodology to achieve them, and a clear indication of when your goals have been completed.

❦

Chapter Fourteen

Supporting: Having Company on Your Journey

As individual as your wealth-creation journey can be, Sisters have to learn that you can't do it alone. Most of us have been afraid to ask for support and help, and are often beat up, worn down, and too tired to be our queenly selves. Asking for help doesn't mean you are weak, it indicates that you want to remain strong. You have to be willing to share yourself and to be open to receiving the contributions that others can make to your life.

Most of us are afraid to share our ideas, hopes, and dreams because we fear other people will laugh at us, tell us it won't work, or perhaps steal them. You may have these fears because you have not surrounded yourself with the right people. We have all been taken advantage of at one time or another, but we can change that by building a supportive network around us. This network should consist of people who want success for us as badly as we want it for ourselves; people who are going to be there when we need them; people who see the greatness in us when we may not be able to see the greatness in ourselves; people who are going to hold us accountable for whom we say we want to be; people who will love us unconditionally; people who will not judge us, but encourage us or just listen to us when we need a sympathetic ear.

With all the work you have done so far, you are probably enlightened enough to be one of these people yourself. (You can be supportive of another Sister because you know her struggles, pains, fears, hopes, and dreams.)

A support team will help you achieve your dreams. Support comes in various ways, shapes, and forms from people, places, and things. Some people in your support network you establish can be: Lovers, Challengers, Backers, Role Models, Friends, Mentors, Mentees, Like-Minded People, Opposites, Allies, Coaches, and Celebrators.

Lovers are there for you and love you no matter what. This is beyond romantic love. Lovers can be men, women, old friends and new. These are the people who love and accept you for who and what you are. They expect nothing from you; they just love you because you're you.

Challengers demand more from you. In an old mindset you may have considered them the negative or difficult people in your life. They may be difficult to deal with because they confront you, contest or question your opinions, and dispute your reasons. They may be taxing on your nerves. But when you listen and learn from them, they can help you overcome obstacles you may not have been aware of. Challengers help you make continuous improvements in your products, processes, and personal growth.

Backers provide support for your ideas or ventures. They may contribute in monetary or nonmonetary ways. They furnish information and supply you with resources. Backers might be your first customer to show their support. They help to sustain you in ways that you cannot sustain yourself. Backers might be a financial planner, accountant, stockbroker, lawyer, or spiritual leader.

Role Models are people you might like to emulate. Perhaps they have been successful in areas where you want to be successful. A Role Model may be someone you have read about but don't know. They are a source of inspiration.

Friends are your buddies, companions, pals, and confidants. They are the people you have fun with. You like to do the same things and enjoy being in one another's company. You can count on them and they can count on you. You enjoy simple pleasures with them like shopping, eating, discussing books and what you're doing Saturday night.

Mentors, unlike Role Models, consciously help you along your journey. They have knowledge, experience, wisdom, and resources in specific areas that they willingly share with you. They may be older or younger. For this relationship to be beneficial for you both, you have to be willing to be a mentee or protégée.

Mentees or protégées may be either yourself or people who help you by allowing you to help them. They are people you have committed to help by sharing your knowledge, experience, wisdom, and resources. You can clarify your points of view by answering their questions. This relationship helps you to rethink and refine your beliefs and preferences.

Like-Minded People share your goals, aspirations, or political, religious, or spiritual beliefs. These relationships may be long-term or short-term. A Like-Minded Person may be someone in a class with you, someone you work out with at the gym, someone you met at Weight Watcher's, or someone you met at church. You have something in common, and you enjoy having that person in your support system for that reason. You may or may not be personal friends.

Opposites are people who are different from you. You appreciate them for the diversity of their views and opinions. They aren't like you, nor do they want to be like you. They like who they are and they like who you are. They open up new possibilities and new paradigms for you. They introduce new perspectives into your life.

Allies are your advocates. They stand up for you and your point of view. They cover your back. They may be your collaborators or your partners on projects.

Coaches help you chart your behavior, not based upon your past, but upon what you want for the future. They tell it like it is, even though the truth may be difficult to hear. They help you determine "what's missing" and develop a plan to get the missing piece of the puzzle. They allow you to try out what they're saying and disregard it if it doesn't fit or work out. They allow you to choose what you're going to do. For a coaching relationship to be successful, you have to be coachable by requesting and accepting help.

Celebrators applaud, cheer, honor, and rejoice in your achievements and successes—great or small. They are happy because you are happy, and they let you know it.

The kind of support you may have been used to in the past came from people who agree with you, no matter what. You're beyond that now. Also, you may have tried to get all of your support from one person, perhaps your significant other or a parent. It's not fair to expect all of your support to come from one source. As you grow and evolve, sometimes you outgrow your supporters in certain areas, which may mean it's time to move on.

To gain the support of others, you have to share what you are doing, so they can step in and assist. It is important not to keep all of your goals and aspirations to yourself. When you are expressing yourself authentically and naturally, you will begin to live your life fully. You will get what you need to attain what you want.

You cannot help other Sisters unless you are continuously working on yourself, doing inner and outer work. We are all on a journey together, not only to support ourselves, our families, and our community, but also to leave a legacy for those who follow.

You can support others in creating new possibilities for their lives and in making those possibilities happen. You need to sincerely want to lend a helping hand. Not just because it's the political thing to do, but because your spirit tells you it's the right thing to do. Give people hope and help them create their futures. Provide leadership for others. Communicate in a way that inspires and calls for the alignment, cooperation, and partnership of others. You can do this when you are clear about what you want and what you want to accomplish. When people see that you want to make a contribution to others, they will support you.

Develop your ability to express yourself, your thinking, and your ideas effectively. If you are seeking the participation, enthusiasm, and support of those around you, you don't want to obscure your message with doubt, powerlessness, embarrassment, or self-consciousness. You want to be able to express yourself so that others relate to you not from their past experience or opinion of you, but from the power you bring to the present and the possibility you open for the future.

In addition to developing your people support system, there are other things that can assist you in becoming resourceful. These include books, seminars, research, asking questions that will get what you want, and being comfortable asking for help. Interdependence, collaboration, and cooperation with others will get you much further than competitiveness. Consider bartering, leveraging relationships, building teams, and forming strategic alliances to make your dreams come true.

Asking for support and giving support are two sides of the same coin. You may want to invest in someone else's dreams or business. However, don't turn your money over to others unless you know they truly have a wealth-creation consciousness and a business background. People without this knowledge won't be able to make good investments for you, no matter how good their ideas are. Make sure their beliefs and thoughts about money are as much in alignment with yours as possible. Get to know others by working on smaller projects before venturing into more risky business relationships.

If you want to invest in other people's businesses or financially fund their dreams or life's work, be aware that this is a business in itself. It is best to invest in projects and people that are closely aligned with who you are, rather than in projects and people you don't understand. Invest in things you know about and care about.

If you give responsibility for your investments to other people, make sure they have a good understanding of what they are doing and that you have the ability to monitor and evaluate their performance according to your standards. However or wherever you invest your money, stay conscious of what is being done with it and check on it fairly frequently. Think about where you want to be in five, ten, or fifteen years, and invest your money in a way that it becomes a part of your plan to get there.

Look around you. Who are your close friends? Do they have entrepreneurial mind-sets? Can they make a difference in your life? If the answer is "no," what are you doing about it? I remember being told, "You are known by the company you keep." Get out there. Develop dynamic relationships with people who share your mind-set. If you want to be an entrepreneur, hang out with entrepreneurs. I'm not saying drop the friends you have. They have been there for you through thick and thin. I'm suggesting that you add friends, acquaintances, and companions who can support you as you create your future. Where are the people who have accomplished what you want to accomplish? Are you attending networking activities such as conferences, meetings, or churches where you can connect with Sisters who are creating their future?

Consider Creating a *Cashing-In* Team

A *Cashing-In* Team is a group you select and choose to meet with regularly, preferably weekly. The purpose of the meetings is to support each other in accomplishing goals. The team meeting is not a pity party or self-improvement group. It is a system in which each person helps all the others go after their dreams. It could change your view of what's possible for your life. The *Cashing-In* Team is a group of supportive people who believe in you and in the importance of your goals and hold you accountable to stick with it, as if you were doing it for them, not just for yourself. The knowledge that someone is holding you accountable, waiting to hear whether you did what you said you'd do and how it went, is a powerful motivator.

Each week, you will tell the *Cashing-In* Team exactly what steps you are committed to accomplishing for the following week, day by day. Your team will share their commitments with you, too. The next week, you'll report in and tell each other what you did or didn't do, holding each other accountable for the promises and commitments previously made.

The team system works. Your attempts at self-discipline when you work alone are susceptible to procrastination and distraction. When someone else is holding you accountable, it is a lot harder to fool yourself.

The questions that arise in your group will be the same questions you used to ask yourself to test your progress:

What have I accomplished?

What haven't I accomplished?

What's missing?

What's next?

Build a network of people who are honest and competent to give you feedback—in other words, a group of folks who are committed to your commitments. They may be friends; they must be people you will listen to seriously. A *cashing-in* network is an excellent tool to keep you honest and working on your goals.

Chapter Fifteen

Sharing: The More You Give, the More You Get

WE teach others by setting an example. It is hard, if not impossible, to help lead others to wealthy lives if you do not have the feeling of wealth about your own life. You do not want living at a survival level or victim level to be the example you set. When you have the right amount of money and money works in your life, people will learn about wealth by your example. Develop empowering beliefs that will lead you to financial freedom. The more you give to others, the more you will receive on an ongoing basis.

Setting an example means walking the talk, teaching values, and being honest about past financial difficulties and how you overcame them. It requires setting priorities and living from those priorities by the way you manage and budget your money and live your life.

Being wealthy requires a good work ethic, community involvement, a new spirit, new care, new communication, a new attitude, and a new commitment. This challenge offers more opportunity, and the opportunity extends to more of us. But it also demands more time, energy, generosity, and creativity from you.

Often, people get confused about giving and receiving because they wonder how much they should give in order to receive. The way to ensure that you will always have enough is to forget about the money and concentrate on giving of yourself, supporting people, putting out energy, and being there for others. People are scared and insecure, and they need emotional support; they need protection. It costs you nothing to give it to them.

Carol McCall is president of a training firm called World Institute Group of Companies, as well as a dynamic facilitator and author. She captured the essence of sharing when I asked her what success meant to her. She told me, "True success is that which co-creates success in the lives of others. A truly successful individual is not one who has the most personal achievements to claim. He or she is the one who can point to the success of others into whose lives he or she has contributed."

To be a contributor, practice listening, empathizing, really hearing what others say. Look them in the eye when they speak; repeat to them the words they have used, so they know you have listened and understood them. When they are negative, help them turn their negativity around.

Don't buy into their emotion; just be there for them while they let it out. Don't try to fix things. People often need to vent problems to release tension. Be a strong and loving person who listens and empathizes.

Show interest in life and people. When you meet people, ask them questions. Find out what's going on in their lives and how you might contribute to their dreams. Never express disapproval of them or their efforts. You might suggest, in a nonthreatening way, some other course of action—one that might be stronger, more likely to succeed than the course they've embarked on. Never intentionally make them feel small or say things that might hurt or scare them. Always try to keep them safe.

Give emotionally to others, and open yourself up to being there for others. Be kind and generous; never rob people of their positive outlook or their hopes. Build them up; don't tear them down, even if you don't understand or disagree with their ideas. Back them verbally and emotionally, without condition.

Once you have started emotional giving, the rest follows naturally. You can give money and gifts, depending on what you can afford. Sometimes a small gift, carefully chosen with the recipient in mind, is more valuable than something that costs a lot.

Give silently. When you pass people on the street, mentally reach out and touch them in the heart and silently project the thought "love" toward them, or project admiration for them even though you don't know them. Back them. Believe in them. Give them hope. If you see that they are upset, project "serenity" or "calm." If you see that they are angry, project "peace." Don't judge them; know they have some unresolved inner issue, probably from a long time ago. Love them even if you don't find them attractive.

One of the best actions you can perform in relation to giving and receiving is to keep a gratitude book—a journal of all the things you are grateful for. As a discipline, write in it every day and try to find five things each day that you are grateful for. It's a way of sharing your gratitude that draws wealth to you. In the act of being grateful, you are acknowledging your wealth. The fact that you have to take, say, five minutes to write in your journal each day means that you are observing your blessings and making them more real. Your mind projects more satisfaction and less lack. This opens the way for more good things to come to you.

Consider tithing. Tithing is more than financial tithing. Tithing is a commitment to give of your time, talents, or treasures. Tithing establishes a regular method of giving—out of love and joy. It is a self-imposed discipline, and it's the beginning of development of a consciousness centered in God.

Another way of sharing is with and through networks. Sisters can come together to share skills, talents, and experiences; to educate business leaders and other interested groups about women's contributions; to share concerns about issues affecting women in the marketplace; to share their knowledge about subtle ways that women's beliefs impede their success and advancements; and to help business leaders succeed by tapping into women's talents. To do all of this, Sisters work together and form groups of like-minded women who can help each other move their careers, businesses, and organizations forward.

Women need to join together in greater numbers to bring old paradigms into the open and link up with other business leaders, who may be intrapreneurs or entrepreneurs, to develop new paradigms and new agendas for the twenty-first century. This can also be done by advising senior management, human resources, and diversity councils on the issues facing women in your company. You can share by holding meetings for women, setting up mentoring programs and speakers series, and other business development activities. When you share, you improve the environment for women overall.

Being a woman is challenging. We women are concerned about our children, our parents, and ourselves. But you have to remember how important it is to shift your consciousness to love and compassion for others. If you are around people who talk about their financial problems all the time, see if you can help them see ways to empower themselves and generate a wealthy lifestyle.

You have to find others on the same journey and make a strong collective statement about your passions. When an idea reaches critical mass, there is no stopping the shift. You have to honor your feminine qualities of intuition, healing, and peace, and nurture those who are less fortunate. There is freedom, wealth, and power for all Sisters when women share their experiences in formal (professional associations, investment clubs, school career days, etc.) and informal networks (family, friends, co-workers).

The key to your sharing network's success, especially in the first few years, is to make sure you are doing the activities that support what network members want while making a positive contribution to the business community in which the network members share and serve.

In addition to the *Cashing-In* Teams and coaches mentioned earlier, you can share with a Master Mind partner. A Master Mind partner is a person with whom you meet regularly in a spirit of harmony, trust, and love. She listens attentively to the requests you make, and affirms her complete support for you to become and achieve all that your heart desires.

A Master Mind partner is a member of a sharing group. Members of a Master Mind group choose the persons with whom they wish to be in partnership. All existing members of the group must agree upon the admittance of any new partner.

A Master Mind partner is someone to call when you need support or guidance. Master Mind partners remain in close contact with one another, either in person or by telephone. A Master Mind partnership is a community of equals. There is no established leader. A Master Mind partner respects confidentiality. Because of the closeness of a Master Mind alliance, deeply personal facts and feelings may be shared. Each member's ability and willingness to honor those confidences is essential to maintaining the spiritual bond between members and within the group.

Others can benefit from the unique knowledge, skills, experience, and talent that you have. There are many ways you can make your contribution. By sharing yourself with others and with your community, you enrich everyone.

Chapter Sixteen

Shaping the Future: We're All One

TOGETHER, Sisters can help transform the world. Individually, you create your personal experiences based on your beliefs. Virtually everything begins with you, the individual. If you are not transformed, the world cannot be transformed. Together, we can create a better future when, individually and collectively, we understand that the future of the world begins on an individual level, then moves out into our families and communities. Our current beliefs have already shaped the world in which we live today; they are also shaping our future.

WHERE DO YOU BEGIN?

Start by identifying the economic, political, and social conditions in the world that you care most about. Many times, you react most strongly to world problems that reflect your own personal challenges. You won't create wealth for others by denying yourself what you need and want. Remember to love and be generous with yourself. Satisfy your own needs and desires, and you will automatically help others fulfill theirs.

What's next for you? It's up to you. What new possibilities do you see for yourself? What obstacles do you see standing between you and those possibilities?

Awareness is only one small part of *cashing in*. Transformation requires that you do more than analyze, advise, and sermonize; you must take action. To support your process of being in action, do something every day that will bring consistency and discipline into your practices. Do the same thing, preferably at the same time. It doesn't matter whether it's taking a walk, praying, meditating, writing in your journal, or spending time with family and friends, as long as it is an activity that contributes to you and your future.

Commit to what matters to you. Embrace what life serves you rather than resisting it or comparing it with something else. Experience satisfaction while you meet the demands of your commitments. Consider life a game, then choose the game you are committed to, and then surrender to the discipline of that game. When you think about making your financial dreams come true, think about Martin Luther King, Jr., and his dream. What determined his actions (and determines the actions of any committed person) was his dedication to the possibility that his dreams could become reality. Sister, *cashing in* is your reality.

Maintain balance in your life; don't get lopsided or carried away with one aspect to the exclusion of others. Understand your financial situation and determine how much you will need to fulfill your goals. Ask yourself:

What is my vision for my life?

What is my vision for the world?

What are the gifts I bring to the world?

Who are the people in my life who matter to me?

What contributions can I make to them?

Where do I go from here?

You have to be willing to declare unequivocally what you stand for, and to risk the vulnerability that comes with taking such a stand. Be willing to tell the world about your commitments.

Commit yourself to causes that are meaningful to you, that you can embrace wholeheartedly. Then be committed to your commitments, by making decisions according to what will best further them.

Examine your values and concerns; discover what really matters to you. Your commitments have a chance of lasting and being a source of deep fulfillment only if they align with your priorities.

Be rigorous and specific about your words and actions. Back up what you say with what you do. Be honest about the results. What really happens provides the best tangible data for evaluating your effectiveness and for correcting yourself.

The Future

Women are a strong collective force, and it is time for us to become recognized and respected for our excellence and economic contributions. We must be flexible and adaptable to change and transformation. We must be ready to accept the challenges, opportunities, and possibilities awaiting us in the twenty-first century, and adapt and prosper with economic uncertainties.

My prediction for the future is that we women will value our diversity, take racism and sexism and turn them to our advantage, operate from a position of collective power, and consider ourselves a crucial resource for the American economy. The time for us to embrace our power and set our creativity free has at long last arrived. It is not a time for us to hold back; it is time for us to *cash in*. Women will begin to talk with each other and to listen to each other for the power we possess. We will coach and encourage each other. We women will transform the world we live in. We will know each other as Sisters and help men to know what we think so we can collaborate as Sisters and Brothers together.

Sisters who have cashed in will be readily identifiable, highly valued, and respected as partners in helping the national and global economy prosper. Sisters with profitable and successful business enterprises will no longer be exceptions to the rule.

We can have a world where millions of empowered Sisters, from Oprah Winfrey to Oseola McCarty to thirty-nine-year-old Microsoft millionaire retiree Trish Millines, create wealth for ourselves and our communities. We can make the LEAP into the future, get on track, and stay on track during the wealth-creation journey.

You are an integral part of our collective ability to reshape the future. As you and others work individually and collectively, women's financial dreams will come true state by state, city by city, and Sister by Sister.

Resources

BOOKS

Personal Growth and Perspective on Money

Adrienne, Carol. *The Purpose of Your Life: Finding Your Place in the World Using Synchronicity, Intuition, and Uncommon Sense*. New York: Eagle Brook, 1998.

Anderson, Nancy. *Work with Passion: How to Do What You Love for a Living*. New York: Carroll & Graf, 1984.

Anthony, Dr. Robert. *Doing What You Love, Loving What You Do: The Ultimate Key to Personal Happiness and Financial Freedom*. New York: Berkley, 1991.

Breathnach, Sarah Ban. *Something More: Excavating Your Authentic Self*. New York: Warner Books, 1998.

Brown, Les. *Live Your Dreams*. New York: Avon Books, 1996.

Caldwell, Kirbyjon H. *The Gospel of Good Success: A Road Map to Spiritual, Emotional and Financial Wholeness*. New York: Simon & Schuster, 1998.

Dominguez, Joe, and Vicki Robin. *Your Money or Your Life*. New York: Viking, 1992.

Dowling, Collette. *Maxing Out: Why Women Sabotage Their Financial Security*. New York: Little, Brown and Company, 1998.

Ellis, Dave. *Creating Your Future: Five Steps to the Life of Your Dreams*. New York: Houghton Mifflin, 1998.

Eisenson, Marc, Gerri Detweiler, and Nancy Castleman. *Invest in Yourself: Six Secrets to a Rich Life*. New York: John Wiley & Sons, Inc., 1998.

McCarthy, Kevin W. *The On-Purpose Person: Making Your Life Make Sense*. Colorado Springs, CO: Pinon Press, 1992.

Orman, Suze. *The Courage to Be Rich*. New York: Riverhead Books, 1999.

Peterson, David B., and Mary Dee Hicks, Ph.D. *Development FIRST: Strategies for Self-Development*. Minneapolis, MN: Personnel Decisions International, 1995.

Inspiration

Breathnach, Sarah Ban. *Simple Abundance: A Daybook of Comfort and Joy*. New York: Warner, 1995.

Cole, Harriette. *How to Be: Contemporary Etiquette for African Americans*. New York: Simon & Schuster, 1999.

Fortgang, Laura Berman. *Take Yourself to the Top*. New York: Warner, 1998.

McCarty, Oseola. *Simple Wisdom for Rich Living*. Marietta, GA: Longstreet Press, 1998.

Richardson, Cheryl. *Take Time for Your Life: A Personal Coach's Seven-Step Program for Creating the Life You Want*. New York: Broadway, 1998.

Taylor, Susan L. *Lessons in Living*. New York: Doubleday, 1995.

Vanzant, Iyanla. *In the Meantime*. New York: Simon & Schuster, 1996.

Personal Finance/Money Management

Boston, Kelvin. *Smart Money Moves for African Americans*. New York: G. P. Putnam's Sons, 1996.

Ealy, Dr. C. Diane, and Dr. Kay Lesh. *Our Money, Ourselves: Redesigning Your Relationship with Money*. New York: AMACOM/American Management Association, 1999.

Mosbacher, Georgette. *It Takes Money, Honey*. New York: Regan, 1999.

Stephens, Brooke. *Talking Dollars and Making Sense: A Wealth-Building Guide for African-Americans*. New York: McGraw-Hill, 1997.

Career and Professional Development

Bolles, Richard Nelson. *What Color Is Your Parachute?: A Practical Guide for Job-Hunters and Career-Changers*. Berkeley, CA: Ten Speed Press, 1999.

Bridges, William. *Managing Transitions: Making the Most of Change*. New York: Addison-Wesley, 1991.

Profiles/Role Models

Broussard, Cheryl D. *Sister CEO: The Black Woman's Guide to Starting Your Own Business*. New York: Viking Penguin, 1996.

Fraser, George. *Success Runs in Our Race: The Complete Guide to Effective Networking in the African-American Community*. New York: William Morrow and Company, 1994.

Reid-Merritt, Patricia. *Sister Power: How Phenomenal Black Women Are Rising to the Top*. New York: John Wiley & Sons, Inc., 1996.

WORKSHOPS

Coaching, Entrepreneurial Leadership, and other workshops
Making Success Happen, Inc.
http://www.makingsuccesshappen.com

"The Efficacy for Women"
J. Howard & Associates
http://www.jhoward.com/capeff.htm
(781) 862-8887

Personal Development Workshops
Landmark Education Corp.
http://www.landmark-education.com
(415) 882-6300

"Possibility of Woman"
The World Institute Group of Companies
http://listeningprofitsu.com/pow.htm
(502) 895-8904

The "Sisters Are Cashing In" Series and "Resolution 2000"
Various Workshops and Newsletters
http://www.sisterscashingin.com

ORGANIZATIONS

American Association of Individual Investors
(312) 280-0170

Institute of Certified Financial Planners
(800) 282-7526

International Black Summit
P.O. Box 20443
New York, NY 10025

National Association of Black Accountants
(301) 474-NABA (474-6222)

National Association of Black Women Entrepreneurs, Inc.
http://www.NABWE.org
(313) 203-3379

National Association of Investors Corporation
(248) 583-6242

National Association of Negro and Professional Women
(202) 483-4206

National Association of Personal Financial Advisors
(800) 366-2732

National Association of Women Business Owners
(800) 55-NAWBO (556-2926)

National Council of Negro Women
(202) 737-0120

National Coalition of 100 Black Women
(212) 947-2196

INTERNET/WEB SITES

There are many tools available for free on the Internet.
Take advantage of the free tools first to educate yourself
about your situation and to develop a plan that you can
later take to a professional. Here's a list of places for you
to visit for on-line assistance. Remember that Internet
addresses do change and more come on-line every day.
Use a search engine (Infoseek, Lycos, Yahoo, etc.) to
locate old and new sites.

http://www.cccamerica.org/
Credit Counseling Centers of America offers counseling
and debt management services on this site for free. You
can also call 1-800-493-2222 for more information.

http://www.debtorsanonymous.org
The Web site for Debtors Anonymous offers a twelve-step program and a support group for debtors trying to recover from money problems and compulsive spending habits.

http://www.fool.com
Provides information in an educational and sometimes amusing manner to help users understand investing and stocks.

http://www.lycos.com/money/
A site with tools that allow you to calculate car payments, mortgages, retirement, and other budget items for financial planning.

http://www.morebusiness.com
Another business resource center that offers free samples for business agreements, marketing plans, checklists, equipment leases, sales and marketing agreements, living wills, and other planning tools for personal and business finance.

http://www.nccs.org
This site has many tools to help you with budget and finances, from a budget calculator to a debt-to-income work sheet. It is operated by Genus, a nonprofit service offering credit counseling, debt management, and financial education programs. You can contact them at 1-800-210-4455 for additional information.

http://www.nfcc.org

NFCC—The National Foundation for Consumer Credit—is a network of 1,450 nonprofit agencies that provide money management education; confidential budget, credit, and debt counseling; and debt repayment plans for both individuals and families. You can find an NFCC location by calling 1-800-388-2227 (1-800-682-9832 for assistance in Spanish).

http://www.sba.gov

The site for the Small Business Administration offers business plans, start-up kits, work sheets, and other helpful information for aspiring, new, and existing business owners.

http://www.startupbiz.com

This site features a seven-step program for starting a business with a focus on how to trade on your personal knowledge, skills, and talents so that personal growth, not money, will be the biggest payment.

http://www.success.org

Offered by the American Success Institute (ASI), a nonprofit educational organization, this site has on-line assessments that can assist you in determining your goals.

http://www.weightwatchers.com

Weight Watchers is the international organization that has helped millions of women (and men) lose weight and maintain the loss with weight loss plans, menu planning, meetings, and on-line discussion/support groups. You can call 1-800-651-6000 for more information.

On-line Money Management Resources Specifically for Women

I Village: *http://www.ivillagemoneylife.com*

Money Minded: *http://www.moneyminded.com*

WomenConnect: *http://www.womenconnect.com/info/finance*

Women's Wire: *http://www.womenswire.com/money*

Other On-line Resources
Simple Living

Millennium Institute: *http://www.igc.apc.org/millennium/links/simplive.html*

On-Purpose On-line Community: *http://www.on-purpose.com*

The Simple Living Network: *http://www.slnet.com*

Financial Advice

Debt Counselors of America: *http://www.dac.org*

Good Advice Press: *http://www.goodadvicepress.com/links.htm*

Making Success Happen: *http://
www.MakingSuccessHappen.com*

No-Debt Living: *http://www.nodebtnews.com*

E-mail

Marilyn French Hubbard: mfhubbard@sisterscashingin.
com

Index